The
FUTURE
of the African American Church

An INVITATION to Dialogue

Ralph Basui Watkins
Justin G. West

Foreword by Leslie D. Callahan
Afterword by Maisha Handy
Epilogue by Marvin A. McMickle

JUDSON PRESS
PUBLISHERS SINCE 1824
VALLEY FORGE, PA

The Future of the African American Church: An Invitation to Dialogue

Judson Press has made every effort to trace the ownership of all quotes. In the event of a question arising from the use of a quote, we regret any error made and will be pleased to make the necessary correction in future printings and editions of this book.

Scripture quotations are from the following translations:

NIV indicates from the HOLY BIBLE, NEW INTERNATIONAL VERSION®. NIV®. Copyright © 1973, 1978, 1984, 2011 by Biblica, Inc.™ Used by permission. All rights reserved worldwide.

NRSV indicates the New Revised Standard Version Bible, copyright © 1989, Division of Christian Education of the National Council of the Churches of Christ in the United States of America. Used by permission. All rights reserved.

Interior design by Crystal Devine.

Cover design by Wendy Ronga, Hampton Design Group, www.hamptondesigngroup.com.

Library of Congress Cataloging-in-Publication data

The future of the African American church : an invitation to dialogue / Ralph Basui Watkins, Justin G. West.
    pages cm
  ISBN 978-0-8170-1742-2 (pbk. : alk. paper) 1. African American churches. I. Watkins, Ralph Basui, 1962- author. What makes an African American church dead or alive? II. West, Justin G., author. Biblical foundations for ministry in the future of the African American church. III. Watkins, Ralph Basui, 1962- author. Sankofa spirituality. IV. West, Justin G., author. Models of the African American church in conversation. V. Watkins, Ralph Basui, 1962- How to reach and keep what you got. VI. West, Justin G., author. Alive or dead? VII. Watkins, Ralph Basui, 1962- author. Death or resurrection.
  BR563.N4F88 2014
  277.3'08308996073--dc23

                          2013026102

Printed in the U.S.A.

First Edition, 2014.

Contents

Foreword

Throughout the black community, in living rooms, barbershops, and hair salons no less than in vestibules, narthexes, and family life centers, the question of the future of the black church is debated and its outcomes predicted.

Even acknowledging that the narrative that heralds the decline and eventual demise of the church is not new, and that the specific awareness of the challenges of the African American religious expression has been present since W. E. B. DuBois expounded on the "souls of black folk," honest observations about the diminishing participation of young adults on the one hand and the declining cultural salience of religiosity on the other hand could well leave a concerned black Christian wringing her hands and wondering what will become of us.

Church conferences are devoted to the question; pastors ponder it in their studies and in board rooms; concerned lay leaders wrack their brains for a solution to lethargic and unfocused congregational existence, even while outside observers judge the efficacy of black religious life by whatever secular standards they deem appropriate.

What seldom happens though, is what the authors of this book prescribe: namely, the systematic, reasoned, and balanced self-evaluation on the part of *participants* in black Christian communities of their particular forms of Christian expression. As much as we care about our churches, we have difficulty assessing their health and that of our denomination(s) along lines deeper than how much money we raise and how many members we have.

We seem especially inept at accounting for the meaning that cultural and social trends have for us now, let alone estimating their impact on our future prospects. Simply by taking seriously the questions that Watkins and West pose in each of their chapters, pastors, leaders, and lay members can begin to evaluate their congregation's present health and the prognosis for their future wellbeing.

Any of the many kinds of black churches will find something familiar about themselves in this work. Indeed, that is its great strength—that Watkins and West recognize the existence and appreciate the myriad and mixed forms of black church life. From the Introduction, they acknowledge and affirm the spectrum of black churches, from the "praise" to the "prophetic," with an awareness that these ideal types meld and overlap one another, even as the focus of each kind of church has something to teach and contribute to its counterpart.

As a pastor deeply formed and nurtured by the vibrant worship and personally transformative piety characteristic of the "praise" style churches while simultaneously convicted that "prophetic" consciousness about social conditions and systems is a biblical mandate, I am unwilling to concede that either aspect of black Christianity is unnecessary. In fact, it is clear that a diversity of styles and emphases are needed and appropriate to the diversity of needs in community.

And yet even with such useful diversity among African American Christian communities, there are many common issues and challenges that intersect with us all, and I would argue that our future existence and our contemporary relevance will be determined by our navigation of these issues and challenges.

The issues that the authors take up in the last two chapters of the book—issues of gender, family structure, sexuality, and class— might be summarized as a call for the church's examination and affirmation of fundamental humanity, both for its constituents and even for those outside of its communion. As the authors point out, theological and social perspectives might occasion substantial diversity in policy, yet the incapacity of the church to treat people consistently in a fashion that bespeaks loving regard for individual and collective human worth undermines our witness and relevance.

Be they "praise" or "prophetic," our congregations and denominations still have a great deal of work to do to demonstrate practically our acknowledgment of the full humanity of all persons, particularly the women who still make up the majority of our congregations. Feminist/womanist work, then, is not just an interpretative, explanatory

advisable hermeneutical strategy; it is a necessary corrective to the exclusionary theological and political structures of our churches. I am hopeful that the questions—theological, ecclesiological, and practical—that this work raises will indeed prompt the conversations that will bring us to a healthier future. *Related to the study of the church*

Leslie D. Callahan, MDiv, PhD
Pastor, St. Paul's Baptist Church
Philadelphia, Pennsylvania

Introduction

My Story and Our Future: Ralph Basui Watkins

Every book we write, every film we make, every sermon we preach, every lecture we give has some portion of our autobiography in it. This book is no different. I write this book from a peculiar place. While lodging myself in the "prophetic" tradition of the African American religious experience, raised and ordained in the African Methodist Episcopal (AME) Church, I consider myself a son of Bishop Richard Allen, the Reverend Jarena Lee, Bishop Reverdy Ransom, and Bishop Henry McNeal Turner. The major theological influences in my life have been Dr. James Cone, Dr. Kelly Brown Douglas, Dr. Jacquelyn Grant, and Dr. James Hood. My intellectual idols are Dr. Molefi Asante, Dr. W. E. B Du Bois, Dr. Patricia Hill-Collins, and bell hooks.

Moreover, when I really look in the mirror, I see my mother, Earlene Watkins, who nurtured me to be a freedom fighter. When you get to chapter 7, that part of the book where I invite you to think with us about the future of the church, you will understand why I offer a feminist approach; it is my mother who yet speaks to me and through me. It is to my mother, and to generations of strong Christian women who, like her, have formed the backbone and lifeblood of the African American church, that I owe my vision.

Now, let's move to pivotal moment that sparked this present work. It was November 9, 2007, and I found myself sitting across from Bishop Noel Jones, at the Ritz Carlton Hotel in Marina Del Ray California being interviewed for the position of director of ecclesia / executive pastor. Here I was considering a move from First African Methodist Episcopal Church in Los Angeles to come on staff at The City of Refuge where Bishop Jones was the pastor.

What was I doing? What was I thinking? I was firmly established at First AME Church in Los Angeles, known to the world as FAME. FAME was made famous under the leadership of Rev. Cecil "Chip" Murray in the 1990s as they led the city of Los Angeles through the civil unrest during the Rodney King era. From there FAME became the church that was visited by President George W. Bush, President Bill Clinton, Nelson Mandela, and others as FAME became the political center and activist church of the West Coast. When a little-known candidate named Barack Obama visited Southern California for the first time, he came to speak at FAME. So, here I was sitting across from Bishop Noel Jones talking about leaving FAME and coming to The City of Refuge.

These churches couldn't be more dissimilar. Where FAME was an intentionally politically active church, The City of Refuge was not. The City of Refuge was a worship center that prided itself on great music and great preaching. It was a place for the hurting, the rejected, the left out, the put out, the put down, and those who needed revival on Sunday. At The City, as we would call it, many of our members caught the bus to church. It was a mass church, primarily made up of working-class African Americans. In contrast, FAME was a middle- to upper-middle-class church where the majority of members drove to church from around the greater Los Angeles area.

What was drawing me away from FAME and to The City of Refuge? What was drawing me was my appreciation for what The City had to offer. Here was a church that had a great worship experience but a limited ministry footprint. By contrast, FAME was a great church with a well-established ministry footprint and a good worship experience on Sunday. We had good music at FAME, but we hadn't produced gospel albums that were nominated for Stellar Awards, as The City had done. At FAME we had solid preaching, but it wasn't in the same league with the preaching of the legendary Bishop Jones. Bishop T. D. Jakes has called Bishop Jones the greatest preacher in America. When you left worship at The City of Refuge you felt better. Worship made a difference each and every Sunday—but The City was not the same the rest of the week. The place that was a refuge and revival center on Sunday was a wasteland Monday through Saturday, with the sole exception of midweek Bible study, where attendance was typically hit or miss.

At FAME, worship on Sunday was powerful and affecting, but it wasn't in the same league in relationship to what you experienced at The City. Sunday worship at FAME was vibrant, but FAME's more substantial impact was what it did Monday through Saturday. On FAME's sprawling campus there wasn't a day of the week that activity wasn't happening. At FAME housing, more than one thousand low-income Angelinos found affordable housing. FAME Business Development Center served as an incubator for small business, and FAME had a small business loan division that provided venture capital. If you had credit problems they would pray for you at The City, but FAME had a credit management program with counselors who would walk with you through credit repair and help you get back on your feet. If you had legal problems you could visit FAME's legal clinic, where lawyers were waiting to see you after church on Sunday, as well as through the week. While many were crying about the unhealthy condition of the African American community, FAME had a weekly farmers' market where fresh fruits and vegetables were available at reasonable prices. FAME had a health services division, nutrition services, transportation services, and home loans. This was FAME, where the motto was "First to Serve!"

FAME and The City of Refuge were two great churches with very different ministry profiles. They both were meeting a need in the city. They both were making a major difference in the lives of those who called them their church home. What I found during my time at The City of Refuge was that I hadn't appreciated this tradition in the past. I had judged churches like The City of Refuge because they weren't like FAME. What I found after serving at The City was that they were doing something FAME wasn't called or equipped to do. But I discovered that FAME was doing something that The City of Refuge wasn't called to do.

My reflection led me to see that these two congregations met very different needs and ministered to very different populations. They were both needed in our community, for in their own way they provided hope for those who entered their doors. They both were preaching and living the gospel of Jesus Christ in similar yet different ways. They both were relevant to and reflective of the African American religious tradition. What I had come to understand was that my preference of one over the other had led me to judge the one because of my own bias. I had failed to appreciate what I had looked at only from the outside. When I got inside I realized what was really going on. My wife and I would joke after leaving worship at The City of Refuge that Bishop Jones's preaching was so good that I wanted to get saved again. I can't count the Sundays I left The City of Refuge feeling like a new person. The power of that worship experience was overwhelming. I didn't know what this felt like until I had experienced it.

What emerged in me was a dialogue. As I served at The City of Refuge with memories of FAME I began to put these two churches, one prophetic and one praise-oriented, into dialogue. I began to ask questions:

> What would happen if these two churches were in partnership?
> What could they learn from each other?
> How could they support each other?
> How could they share mission, ministry, and members?
> Why is it that they don't talk to each other?
> Do they appreciate each other? Why or why not?
> When could I get these two congregations together?
> What would it look like if FAME and The City of Refuge became one congregation?

What I concluded was that a congregation was not the church but that congregations made up the church. Every congregation could not be all things to all people and do all things. What I began to hope for was a dialogue, a partnership, a relationship, in which congregations that were very different could be in relationship, own their unique mission in relationship to other congregations, share in ministry and vision for a people and community, and see how God could work in this. How could we establish mutually respectful relationships between churches that saw themselves as very different while serving the same God?

This book is an installment in the conversation I dreamed of having between The City of Refuge and FAME. I am in relationship with both The City of Refuge and FAME. I know the pastors and leaders of these congregations well. This book is in many ways your eavesdropping on those conversations I have had with Pastor John Hunter of FAME and Bishop Noel Jones of The City of Refuge.

The future of the African American church is linked to our appreciation of the African American church in all of its various hues. There is no monolithic African American church. There are millions of African Americans congregations, from more prophetic to praise-focused, that make up the African American church. The goal of this book is to put in conversation the various dimensions of the African American church with a hope that we will learn from each other, appreciate each other, and take seriously God's call to us to make a difference in the lives of our people and our community. The book puts the two extreme models of praise and prophetic churches in conversation in hopes that as pastors and church members read this book together they will look at themselves, see themselves in the mirror, and ask what God is calling us to be. How can we learn from each other, partner with each other, and make a real difference in the lives of our people?

My Story and Our Future: Justin G. West

Where do I fit into the story of the African American church? If I were asked to describe in a word my overall experience in the African American church, *complicated* might be the most fitting term. Let me explain why. Throughout my twenty-eight years of life, I have at different times adored, benefitted from, struggled with, and been confused by a number of aspects of the African American church. These sentiments are reflective of a wide range of experiences I have had in both praise and prophetic churches. I have been a part of the Baptist church, a nondenominational but functionally Church of God (Anderson, Indiana) church, and the AME church. I have also participated in the lively worship experiences in storefront churches in Chicago, as well as the Spirit-filled churches in the backwoods of Greenwood, Mississippi, where my grandparents gather.

When I reflect on my diverse experiences in the African American church, I must admit that those experiences have had a defining influence on my life of faith. I cannot deny that I have been blessed again and again and again by the African American church. However, I must quickly confess that there have also been times while I sat in the pews Sunday after Sunday when—despite witnessing energetic preachers perform lively messages that reached the congregation, seeing people get touched by the Spirit and fall out in dancing or convulsions, and observing extremely talented choirs draw the congregation closer to the divine through melodies—I could not help but question the church's relevancy to me—and my relevancy to it.

I found myself asking several critical questions about my relationship with the church as a youngster, a youth, and a young adult. "Is going to church on Sunday mornings really meaningful to me?" "How do some of the strange practices relate to my experience in the present world?" "Am I listening to or observing anything of significant value to my life?" "Could my time be better spent having conversation with my friends over a cup of coffee at Starbucks or at home watching the game?" In other words, I was asking, "Why in the world should *I* go to church?" I didn't always ask this question, but when I did I was in a season of life when church seemed disconnected from my experience in the world.

As I was matriculating inside the African American church, I realized gradually that my frustration with the church was because of a generational and cultural disconnect from past traditions of the African American church. I could not relate to the practices and teachings that had historical significance for my parents, my grandparents, and their parents. I could not relate to the experiences of my parents (who grew up in the Jim Crow South), my grandparents (sharecroppers who lived through the failed Reconstruction), and other African Americans who went to church because it galvanized and enabled them to survive in the face of racism. I grew up in the Midwest, in a suburban and integrated environment that seldom had overt racism. I developed with computers, the Internet, and MySpace in front of me. Naturally, I brought to the table a different set of issues, issues that my elders did not fully know about and/or did not adequately address. I wanted an African American church that spoke to my experience. Where was it?

I slowly became aware that the reason I was disconnected from certain practices in the African American church was mostly because I lacked knowledge, knowledge which resulted in a loss of interest. I lacked knowledge about how certain traditions were meaningful to my elders. I have since learned why the African American church has unique practices. I have learned why it has been important for African American preachers to, as the saying goes, start slow, go slow, go higher, and strike fire in their sermons; I have learned about the significance of "catching" the Holy Ghost "fire" that made a person, to use W. E. B. Du Bois's word, behave in a "frenzy"; and I have learned why my Baptist church in downtown Kansas City would each Sunday sing the old words penned by James Weldon Johnson in 1900:

> God of our weary years, God of our silent tears
> Thou who has brought us thus far on the way
> Thou who has by thy might, led us into the light
> Keep us forever, in the path, we pray.

Learning the value of the preaching and singing of the African American tradition was an educational experience that took time. Nevertheless, even as I learned about and was able to appreciate the history of the African American church, I still couldn't help but wonder about some churches, "When will they say something about the situations I'm facing *today*?"

As a young man who was recently ordained in the AME church, I am still wondering, and I am still concerned. I am concerned because I fear that young adults and youth are still asking the questions I was asking. I am worried because I sense that African American churches of both the praise and the prophetic traditions are stuck in traditions that have become, are becoming, and will become more foreign to younger and future generations. I feel that because younger generations are not finding in some African American churches accommodating social spaces or receiving adequate answers to their questions about life, they remain absent from the pews. I wrestle with the question of how I and other young pastors who are rising up will be able to appreciate different aspects of our traditions but also be catalysts for changes that will bless our generations. How will we do this when pastors or elders who are sixty years of age and older still hold complete control and squelch voices who object to their opinions? Should we leave the African American church in which we developed to start new churches, as many of my peers have done, or should we stay and hope, pray, and strive to initiate change?

Let me share one story with you that illustrates to the need for change. At the church where I attended and served on the ministerial staff as a licentiate, I had an interesting encounter with a young lady one Wednesday night. On Wednesday nights, I had the privilege and responsibility of teaching a youth Bible study before the youth go across the church's parking lot to choir rehearsal. On one night after we had finished our lesson and the youth were getting ready to leave, one youth (whom we'll call Sarah) who had not been present for the Bible study appeared in the doorway. Upon seeing her, another youth in the classroom asked, "Why didn't you come to Bible study?" She responded sharply and emphatically, "I don't do Bible study. I just don't do it." She shook her head, turned, and left.

Not only did I discover that Sarah did not "do" Bible study, but, based on how often I saw her at church on Sunday, she did not do church either. In fact, it seems to me that the only time I noticed her was on the third Sundays when the youth choir would sing and occasionally on Wednesday nights for choir rehearsal. There was something about church that did not vibe well with her. And so she chose not to come.

As I think about our church demographics and practices, though, I cannot blame her lack of interest. I have a good sense of why she didn't come. We had a congregation whose members are primarily over sixty and who prefer the pastor to wear a robe and hymns to be sung. No wonder she came only on the third Sundays, when people dressed down and more up-tempo music was played. Sarah's trend is becoming more and more common among younger generations in some churches. Many youth and young adults show up only on Sundays when they can be sure that the setting and service will be relevant to them. Youth know that on the third Sundays they do not have to feel pressured into dressing up and that there will be upbeat music.

I enter the discussions in this book with Sarah, many other youth and young adults, and my experiences in mind. I am compelled to consider how both praise and prophetic churches, both no doubt steeped in the African American experience, can create an atmosphere where Sarah wants to stay and grow. I want to explore with you ways that our churches can reach and keep generations who are glued to the Web, are developing under a "black" president, and who have Soldier Boy, Black Eyed Peas, Trey Songz, Rihanna, and maybe even Lady Gaga all rotating on their iPods. In a sense, I want to probe how our churches can teach these generations about traditions, like the historical importance of "Lift Every Voice and Sing," while collectively using our minds to write new anthems that minister to the past and present experiences of African Americans.

The Future of African American Churches

What is the future of African American churches? To attempt to answer the question is a bold proposal but nevertheless undertaken with sincere humility. We don't claim to have a crystal ball, but we do claim to have access to a God who is pushing us to engage in a conversation about the future of African American churches. In this work we don't come with corrective prescriptions looking down on African American churches. We come to this conversation as Christians who love the African American church and have served the church all of our adult lives. We are committed to the African American church, as it is our family; this is a family conversation. As we engage in the process of reflection, we envision the family sitting around the kitchen table talking about the church. If you have been a member of an African American church, you know what is like to come home after worship on a Sunday, have Sunday dinner, and talk about the church. We talk about the pastor, the sermon, the choir, the ushers, and anybody in the congregation who deserves to be on our conversational agenda. This project is meant to be an outline for a structured conversation about the future of the churches we love.

We don't want to talk about what the African American church should be; rather, we want to talk about what the African American church can be. We look back at our shinning moments, when we have risen to meet challenges, dealt with crises, led movements, and made a difference. We will use these moments as a testimony of what the church has been and can be without imposing the past as a model for the future. You can't talk about the now without understanding the past, and you can't see the future if you don't expose the connection between the past and the present, which is the foundation for the future.

When we talk about shinning moments in the life of the church, we are not just talking about those times when the church led major social movements; we are also referring to those Sundays when we had good church. Good church can get you through a bad week. Good singing, good preaching, and fellowship make a difference in substantive ways when you are trying to get through what you are going through. We don't draw a tense polemic between the prophetic African American church and what is currently being tagged as the prosperity gospel or praise churches. We will argue that all of the variant strands of the African American church have something of value to offer. Moreover, we will argue that when these various manifestations of the African American church are put in conversation, they each have something to offer the other.

The larger African American church needs sustained reflection over a period of time in various communities, as we collectively assess the state of the church in context and then collectively chart a course for the future of African American churches. For this future-oriented conversation to move forward, this book is supported by a series of videos that will aid in facilitating this conversation. This book and supporting videos are meant to spur on the conversation. (See https://vimeo.com/channels/163594 to view the videos.)

The voices leading the conversation are credible, but we haven't succeeded in getting this conversation into the heart of church life, in congregations where this question must be dealt with. We quickly review the present state of the conversation in order to situate this project. We will look at the work of Marvin McMickle, Eddie Glaude, and Anthony Pinn. Marvin McMickle and Eddie Glaude argue for the prophetic church. The very title of McMickle's book shows his hand: *Where Have All the Prophets Gone? Reclaiming Prophetic Preaching in America*. McMickle sees prophetic preaching and prophetic churches as fighting against injustice in society. But he has harsh words for televangelists and what he calls "megachurces with a mini gospel." McMickle says,

> There is ample emphasis on praise and worship and celebration and feeling good; however, there is scarcely a word about duty or discipleship or self-denial for the sake of others. Such churches need an immediate and intense exposure to Amos 5:23-24 where God announces that songs of praise and shouts of celebration in worship are unacceptable if they are not accompanied by works of justice and righteousness.[1]

Although we sympathize with McMickle, we also hear in his writing almost a disdain for churches that lean toward a praise and worship motif. His concerns are legitimate, but his inability to put praise and worship churches in dialogue with prophetic churches exacerbates the very problem he exposes. How can the praise and worship churches hear his message when he doesn't affirm their ministry? Although his message of the prophetic is right on, his characterization of praise and worship churches is a caricature. We embrace the message of McMickle while showing an appreciation for both ends of the continuum—from praise and worship to prophetic—and we hope to show how they can inform each other.

We seek to make an honest assessment of both forms of the church and to put them in dialogue while not privileging one over the others. We will put on the table the questions that McMickle fails to ask, for example:

Is praise and worship a type of liberative work?
Do praise and worship churches work to set people free?
Is praise and worship a prelude to social justice?
What can prophetic churches learn from praise and worship churches, and vice versa?
What biblical text can put these two models in conversation instead of pitting one against the other?

In his so-called obituary for the African American church, Eddie Glaude Jr. says, "Black churches and preachers must find their prophetic voices. . . . And in doing so, black churches will rise again."[2] It appears that Glaude joins the chorus with McMickle that this one model, the prophetic model, represents the best of the African American church, and the church must follow this model. We argue vigorously against such dichotomous thinking. Churches that are labeled as praise and worship churches have something to offer the African American religious experience. The growth of these churches is a sign that they are meeting a need in African American communities. Praise and worship churches that are also grounded in good preaching are serving as centers of liberation from the cares of the world for so many African Americans who have felt the brunt of the recession. Good church on Sunday is a balm for them, a healing and soothing agent. Although McMickle and Glaude critique praise and worship for an absence of social justice focus, they could turn and critique the social justice/prophetic churches for being weak in the area of praise and worship. Although we can refer to these two extremes for the sake of conversation, we can't say it strongly enough that no church is any one type.

Anthony Pinn's *Understanding and Transforming the Black Church* also needs to be a part of our conversation, and those like Pinn need to be heard. Pinn argues that "the purpose of scholarship on Black churches is not the affirmation of those churches, but rather a high level of discourse meant to address the nature and meaning of those institutions. In turn, churches might use this information to further refine their thought and practice."[3] We like Pinn's call, as he suggests that our work should lead the church in a conversation about the nature and meaning of the church. We disagree with him that it is either critique or affirmation.

We are not positioned as Pinn, who represents the outsider looking in; we are the insiders looking out and around. We think engaged scholars who are a part of the conversation about the African American church must be engaged participants in the life of the church and speak frankly out of their contemporary experience in the church while having a vested interest in the future of the African American church. The work of preacher-scholars is to have a witness that supports them in their conversation about the African American church. There aren't high conversations among scholars and low conversations of others, as Pinn suggests. Rather, we argue that we need multiple conversations in communities around the country in the church about the church. These aren't conversations carried out solely in the academy by academicians who aren't central to the life of the church on a daily, Sunday-to-Sunday basis. We firmly believe that our conversation has to be a mix of affirmation and critique, reflective and practical, historical and contemporary, and there are things worthy of affirmation and things that are a cause for pause.

The Central Question

How does the African American church serve the present age? How does the church equip itself to be what it is called to be in 2025 and beyond? To begin a conversation around these questions, we have to extend the work that has been done on African American church growth. Donald Hilliard's *Church Growth from an African American Perspective* (Judson Press, 2006) deals with inner-church dynamics of growing a healthy church, but it doesn't begin to address how we do church in the digital age. Hilliard's book extended the conversation of James Stallings's *Telling the Story: Evangelism in Black Churches* and Preston Robert Washington's *God's Transforming Spirit: Black Church Renewal*, both published by Judson Press in 1988, so we have two texts written in 1988 and one in 2006. And while all three dealt effectively with church growth, there is no way they could have dealt with what we are encountering since the full-scale development of the Internet, with social media and the barrage of YouTube, Vimeo, Twitter, and Flickr, and other sources of Internet activity too numerous to name. The texts of yesterday have something to say about the life of the church, but they have nothing to say about the cataclysmic cultural shift now experienced that we call the digital age.

We deal with the issues that Stallings, Washington, and even Hilliard couldn't have predicted. This book talks about the new type of Christians emerging in the digital age: young Christians in their twenties who aren't denominationally loyal, don't see the institutionalized church as the primary place of spiritual nurture, see other texts as sacred along with the Bible, use social media as their primary tools of communication and learning, and don't have hardwired home phones. They text and produce their own videos, pictures, and Web pages to tell the world who they are. They are Linkedin without being hooked up; they are putting off marriage, living with persons of the opposite sex without the benefit of marriage, supportive of same-sex marriage, and questioning the relevance of historical African American churches.

These new Christians are demanding a church that is transparent, relevant, and engaging of Scripture while being a reflection of Scripture. They are activist-minded but waiting on a cause to rally behind. They are post–civil rights, post–hip hop, and post–Barack Obama and post–Tea Party. They have witnessed the United States elect an African American president, and then have seen how America's most conservative wings have reacted to the election of their president. They grew up watching T. D. Jakes and Eddie Long, and now they are dealing with Bishop Long's possible downfall. This very broadly defined young adult population represents the future of African American churches. Do we understand them, and how will we of the bridge generation work with them to build that future?

Notes

1. Marvin McMickle, *Where Have All the Prophets Gone? Reclaiming Prophetic Preaching in America* (Cleveland: Pilgrim Press, 2006), 81.

2. Eddie Glaude Jr., "The Black Church Is Dead," http://www.huffingtonpost.com/eddie-glaude-jr-phd/the-black-church-is-dead_b_473815.html (accessed October 21, 2013).

3. Anthony B. Pinn, *Understanding and Transforming the Black Church* (Eugene, OR: Cascade, 2009), xvii.

1

What Makes an African American Church Dead or Alive?

RALPH BASUI WATKINS

On February 24, 2010, at 10:18 a.m. Eastern Standard Time, Dr. Eddie Glaude, the William S. Todd Professor of Religion and chair of the Center for African American Studies at Princeton University, morphed into a coroner when he pronounced that the black church was dead. Dr. Glaude wrote, "The Black Church, as we have known it or imagined it, is dead . . . the idea of this venerable institution as central to black life and as a repository for the social and moral conscience of the nation has but disappeared."[1]

The black church is dead! What was the cause of death? According to Dr. Glaude, coroner and professor, the cause of death was differentiation in the African American community, which for him means that the African American community is sociogeographically dispersed in cities and African American churches are in competition with white churches for African American members. Not only are African American churches in competition with white churches; they are also competing in a world where the sacred is no longer under the sole purview of the African American Christian church. African Americans are looking at other traditions and means to express their spirituality and connect with God.

Dr. Glaude claimed that the black church has lost its prophetic voice and isn't speaking out on social issues or being that "moral conscience" that it had been in the past. The black church has been caught, according to Glaude, looking back at its past through rose-colored glasses rather than dealing with the social crisis the African American community is facing today. The critical nexus between life and death, for Glaude, is the absence of what he calls the prophetic voice, which he goes on to claim is the root cause of the black churches' irrelevance. According to Dr. Glaude, African American churches have large gatherings across the country that are, at best, financial empowerment conferences for the attendees, and, at worst, no more than fundraising opportunities for the sponsoring ministries and their leaders. Dr. Glaude asks where the protests are in response to the social ills that are literally killing African American communities. The last line of the death certificate suggests that, at this moment of death, there is the possibility of resurrection, if and when the African American church reclaims its prophetic voice and witness. In essence Dr. Glaude wrote both a death certificate and an obituary.

Reaction to the Obituary

Dr. Glaude's obituary has done what it intended to do, which was to make us look at the African American church and to ask, Are we dead or alive? His work has moved us into a conversation, but I'm not sure if it moved us into action. Action on behalf of the millions of African American congregations across the nation will mean taking the questions Dr. Glaude has raised and wrestling with them in terms of our biblical reflection, our historical legacy, and our present call to witness. It will mean beginning to reform or revolutionize our churches to be what God would have them to be in this age.

The church is called to be the bride of Christ, a living witness of Christ in the world. What should that bride look like in the twenty-first century? In this chapter, we want to ask a series of questions that will help us have a conversation that will propel us into becoming that relevant African American church in the twenty-first century. It is our goal to invite congregations into conversation, not simply for conversation's sake but to move them to reflect and act with us as we walk together as we become that church that God would have us to be in this present age. We are calling the church to reframe and reclaim its mission to be the bride of Christ. As we enter this conversation we want to delve deeper into the core question that Dr. Glaude's obituary raises while focusing on the central question, which for us is, What makes a church dead or alive?

Let us say at the outset that there is no one way to be the African American church. The African American church is diverse—in worship styles, mission priorities, and ministry strengths. Churches are also diverse in terms of socioeconomic demographics and cultural expression. On one end of the continuum are praise churches; on this end of the continuum we find churches that are steeped in great preaching and powerful worship. On the other end of the continuum are prophetic or social activist churches; these congregations have a strong community ministry profile, excelling at outreach, feeding programs, and addressing social issues in their communities, and tend to be very active Monday through Friday.

On both ends of the continuum, and throughout the span of the continuum, there are signs of life and death. We want to think of the African American church across the spectrum from large cathedrals to storefronts. Although we present these two ends of the continuum from praise churches to social activist churches, we want to add a caveat that these types of churches are used for conversational purposes; no church is a true type but more of a mixture. The point of the two extremes of the continuum is to give us some reference points and frames for our conversation.

What Does It Mean to Be the Church?

Before we move forward I want to establish a baseline definition for conversational purposes of what it means to be the church. (Justin will expand this definition in chapter 2.) The church is the body of Christ (1 Corinthians 12:27). Because the church is the body of Christ, we are the expression, the living witness of Christ on earth. Being the body of Christ means that Christ is the head (Colossians 1:18). The church should reflect Jesus as Jesus left witness in Matthew, Mark, Luke, John, and Acts.

Jesus was a healer. Jesus preached and taught in such a way that his teachings were relevant. By relevant we mean his teaching and preaching related to people's real-life situations, and as result of his teaching the people were touched, empowered to live, and ultimately transformed as they followed the way of Jesus. Jesus met people where they were; he didn't judge them or preach down to them based on their life circumstances. Jesus never walked by a hurting person, but rather Jesus stopped and met that person's need. Jesus

17

fed the hungry, healed the sick, took care of widows, and recognized the little things and little people. Jesus sat and talked with sinners; in fact, Jesus was criticized for sitting and eating with sinners. Sinners were those whom the mainstream religious leaders of the day considered to be outside the mainstream. Jesus was also in the streets and in the homes of those with whom he was in relationship. Jesus spent more time in the streets and in people's homes than he did in the temple. One of the most memorable moments of Jesus' ministry was his going into the temple and getting angry at religious people as he turned over tables (Matthew 21:11-13; Mark 11:14-16; John 2:14-16) and drove the moneychangers out with a whip.

To be the church means to be an extension and reflection of the ministry of Jesus. A litmus test for any church is how seriously that church takes the ministry of Jesus. If your congregation read the Gospels (Matthew, Mark, Luke, and John), asked what Jesus was all about during his ministry, and then extended that question by asking, Do we reflect that Jesus in our ministry?, what would the answer be?

What Is the Difference Between Having Church and Being the Church?

Does your church take Jesus' ministry and witness as a model for ministry? Although many churches focus on the Sunday morning experience as the equivalent of being the church because they are having church or worship services, Jesus didn't participate in these types of events and then rest in them as the definition of what he was called to do. Although we are called to assemble together and worship God, Jesus wouldn't say having church is synonymous with being the church. Jesus was a restless Savior who was on the move making a real difference in the lives of the people with whom he came in contact.

Is your church making a real difference in the lives of the people who are members of your congregation and those who are not members whom we pass on our way to worship? How do you know you are making a real difference? Do we see Jesus in your church Monday through Saturday? Does the community outside the four walls of your church see Jesus in the streets, the home, the common places, the coffee shops, the malls, the schools, the jails, the library, athletic events, community events, in the virtual world of the Internet, and in the world of social media making a difference? To be the church is to be truly like Jesus.

We will wrestle more with these questions as we progress in this conversation, but we want to put the issue on the table as we start our reflection. Glaude and many scholars want to frame Jesus as being primarily prophetic, but I would argue that Jesus was holistic in his approach to ministry. The real question for the church is, How seriously do we take Jesus?

What Does It Mean to Be an Alive African American Church?

As we move from the larger discussion, which we return to in the next chapter, let's get back to the issue at hand: What does it mean to be an alive African American church? Dr. Gayraud Wilmore starts us off as he defines what we mean by blackness and how we are to live out what it means to be black or African American in the context of our religious tradition:

> As applied to religious institutions blackness came to mean the renewal and enhancement of the most esteemed values of African American spirituality; the search for distinctive characteristics of African and African American religions; the refusal to accept Euro-American history, theology, liturgy, and ecclesiastical infrastructures as normative; and a historic vocation to serve and promote the social, economic, and political well-being of the African American community.[2]

According to Wilmore, to be an African American church means that we value the heritage of African American spirituality. Vibrant African American churches are rooted in and connected to the spirit of Africa and the Spirit's traveling down through the ages. An alive African American church celebrates how the Holy Spirit has been manifested in black churches. We hold onto and celebrate the shout, the dance, the ecstatic, and the demonstrative while finding ourselves being moved by the liberative initiation of the Holy Spirit. It was the Holy Spirit who informed our moves toward social justice. It was the Holy Spirit who empowered us to speak truth to power.

The Holy Spirit informed our preaching, inspired our singing, and breathed life through the voices of our choirs. It was the Holy Spirit who met us at worship and made our feet pat and hands clap, and it was that same Spirit who called us to quiet contemplation, to think, reflect, study, and act. African American churches that call themselves alive continue to celebrate the spiritual heritage of the African American tradition.

Second, Wilmore pushes us to think about how African American churches maintain a stance of being countercultural in relationship to the dominant Euro-American culture. African American churches aren't seduced by the process and power of socialization that leads to assimilation and thereby lose their distinctive character of what it means to be an African American church. To be countercultural means that African American churches stand against the seduction of capitalistic greed and cultural assimilation. African American churches are not trying to be simply American, but rather they are trying to hold onto and celebrate what it means to be both African and American.

This distinctive nature calls on the African American church to love its people and cultural heritage. This is not a love in opposition to others. It is not a love that says to love me means I can't love other people or other ethnic groups. This is a love that says if I don't love me, as black as I am, then I can't love others. To love being black is to be empowered to love others while celebrating the Creator's design in blackness. God made us with brown skin and black hair along with cultural norms rooted in our African genesis. Our roots are what keep us anchored as we celebrate our heritage. We are to bask in our distinctive nature with no apologies. From a sociopsychological perspective we are saying that African American churches that are alive teach African Americans to love themselves.

African American churches develop healthy personalities among their members and the community. A healthy black or African American personality is "characterized by a strong awareness of and identification with African cultural heritage, a strong sense of motivation directed in insuring the collective survival of African people and related institutions, and the active resistance of any force (i.e., racism) that threatens the survival and maintenance of one's people and oneself."[3] When African American churches are focused on developing healthy African American personalities, their programs, ministry, worship, and outreach all seek to affirm the blackness of their people.

Alive African American churches hold to that biblical standard that you can't love others until you first love yourself and your God. African Americans receive so many negative images and messages about themselves in the larger culture; in contrast, the African American church provides an alternative message rooted in the African roots of our faith as the church teaches African Americans to love themselves. We celebrate the fact that our Jesus comes from Africa, as the Bible says in Matthew 2:15: "Out of Egypt [Africa] I have called my son." The great history of Africa and the ability of people of African descent to thrive in the midst of brutal conditions throughout our long history helps us realize that we have a lot to be proud of and we should hold our heads up. African American churches make sure their members hold their heads up.

Finally, Wilmore suggests that to be a black or African American church means that as a congregation you work for and on behalf of the interest and concerns of your members and community. The things that plague your members and community as a result of being members of a minority group are your concern. Sociologically speaking, members of minority groups are so designated because they experience collective discrimination as a result of being a member of that group. Therefore African Americans have experienced discrimination simply because they are African American, and when we add class status and gender to the experience, the discrimination becomes more brutal.

Wilmore suggests that an African American church is called by God to act and respond by fighting against discrimination. African American churches seek to understand how systemic discrimination works. They understand the larger issues of systemic discrimination, and they work via direct action to dismantle the systems that thrive as a result of oppressing African Americans. African American churches aren't fooled by the Horatio Alger myth that anyone can make it in America. African American churches know that the Horatio Alger myth is a story contrived by the forenamed author. African American churches understand that in a stratified society the deck is stacked against the have-nots, and African American churches work tirelessly to overthrow an abusive system that is built on the backs of their people.

Freed and Freeing: Living Out of the Struggle

In essence the African American church is meant to be an agent of freedom for African Americans as the church engages in the mission of holistic salvation. We need to take a moment to define what we mean by holistic salvation. When we take seriously Jesus' cry in Luke 4:18, we see that Jesus was clear that salvation is about setting people free from all forms of oppression. Jesus proclaims that he was sent both to preach (spiritual) and to release the oppressed (physical). In the eyes of Jesus, these two aims weren't mutually exclusive but rather were inextricably linked.

To understand fully the meaning of salvation it must be connected to how salvation has manifested itself through the liberating acts of God in Scripture. If we look at Exodus 15:1-3, God intervenes in history to set God's people free. Their liberation from Egypt wasn't limited to a spiritual liberation, but God came to set them free literally. As we look at God as God acts in history and instructs us to act in the present, God's view of salvation is both spiritual and physical.

James Cone has said, "Whenever theology defines the gospel independently of liberation (i.e., independently of social, economic, and political freedom), it is planting the seed that separates spiritual freedom from physical freedom. Unfortunately, Euro-American theology is famous for making the distinction between the physical and the spiritual."[4] African American churches that refuse to allow Eurocentric theology to dominate their theology reject a view of salvation that disconnects the physical and the spiritual. African American churches are as vigilant about Romans 10:9, which calls us to confess Jesus Christ as Lord and Savior, as they are about Matthew 25:31-46, which calls us to serve, meet needs, and transform communities as we serve the least of these.

An alive African American church also has an ethnic and cultural component. (For the purposes of this book, we consider that when the majority of your members are African American and a majority of leaders in the church are African American, this constitutes the benchmark to be classified as an African American church.) This ethnic component informs the cultural and missional component in that to be a part of the African American religious experience suggests that the cultural norms of the African American community are also present in your church.

According to W. E. B. Du Bois, who wrote *The Souls of Black Folk* in 1903, it was the preaching, the frenzy, the music, and the power of the Spirit that made African American churches. I would argue that his analysis is still worthy of our consideration today.

> The Preacher is the most unique personality developed by the Negro on American soil. A leader, a politician, an orator, a "boss," an intriguer, an idealist—all these he is, and ever, too, the centre of a group of men . . . The music . . . Sprung from the African forest, where its counterpart can still be heard, it was adapted, changed, and intensified by the tragic soul-life of the slave until, under stress of law and whip, it became the one true expression of a people's sorrow, despair, and hope. . . .

> Finally the Frenzy or "Shouting," when the Spirit of the Lord passed by, and, seizing the devotee, made him mad with supernatural joy, was the last essential of Negro religion and the one more devoutly believed in than all the rest. . . . And so firm a hold did it have on the Negro, that many generations firmly believed that without this visible manifestation of God there could be no true communion with the invisible.[5]

Does the preaching or teaching in your church come out of and speak to the continuing project of liberation for African Americans who struggle against oppression and discrimination? Does your church make room for the frenzy or the work of the Holy Spirit? And does the music in your church come out of and speak to the African American experience, or are you singing songs written from outside your culture that have little to do with the struggles and victories that African Americans experience as members of a minority group in America?

Alive black churches recognize and listen to the women in the church because the women have been and continue to be our leaders. Of course, women have not always been given the credit for their leadership because we tend to look to the pulpit and not the pew as the center of the church. As Cheryl Townsend Gilkes points out, "Because the preacher was so often 'he,' there was a failure to take seriously all the effective leadership voices, male and female, that were both *performative* and strategic."[6] Alive churches recognize these voices that lead the church from the pew to the pulpit, female and male.

Remember when Du Bois talked about the frenzy? Gilkes calls our attention to the fact that, "Du Bois's frenzy was the community's expression of its engagement with the holy and the voice Du Bois presented was a woman's. Almost no one has pointed to the gendering of that voice, which represents the community engaged with and under the authority of the Spirit. However, it was a woman's voice that was the soul of the folk..."[7] An alive black church hears the voice of God via the community and pays special attention to the role of women as the foundation of the church.

While the leadership and support of women in the life of the church have sustained the church over the years, we can't assume that their support is based on uncritical satisfaction with the church. Daphne Wiggins wrote, "Male clergy assume that women's participation suggests their concerns are satisfactorily addressed and that the church is faring well by this constituency. This perception, however, might be only part of the truth."[8] Wiggins calls churches to interrogate the presence of women and get the other part of the truth. Is the church addressing the liberative needs for African American women? What are the needs of African American women? To what extent is the church empowering women to lead in all aspects of ministry, from the usher board to the pulpit? How are we endeavoring to exorcise our churches of the demon of sexism?

In Touch with History with an Eye on the Future

To be an alive African American church means that you are in touch and in tune with African American history and that you celebrate how God has been and continues to be a means of liberation for our people. African American churches are steeped in praise, and they are praising God for making a way out of no way while simultaneously calling attention to the continued systemic oppression their people face.

We are in no way trying to limit the African American experience to one that is solely defined by oppression, because the cry of the oppressed has resulted in forms of liberation throughout our history. While African Americans have had liberative breakthroughs throughout our history, these moments have been followed by new forms of oppression. Thus, we must develop new ways of overcoming struggle in order to dismantle those forces that seek to reincarcerate our people, including oppressive policies and systems. While we celebrate those moments in our history where God has acted as a liberative God, we don't want to overlook the work of liberation that is yet to be completed.

African American churches are concerned about and speak to the issues of the digital divide, poverty, sexism, overcrowded–underfunded–understaffed public schools, the prison industrial complex, the lack of access to healthcare, residential redlining, the concentration of poverty in inner cities and in rural America, the socioeconomic divide within the African American community between the haves and the have-nots, and the inherent oppression in a stratified society. While speaking out about the African American experience, the church lifts up and encourages our people to take a stand and act to reassure our people that God has not forsaken us. An alive African American church takes real action that makes a real difference as evidence that God is working.

Black preaching is preaching that empowers African Americans to shout in the midst of the storm. It is out of life experience and in the context of worship that the living Word, in the art of preaching, is confirmed. In the African American experience, worship is efficacious. Worship can be ecstatic and high in the spirit or quiet and comforting, but it is always a personal encounter as African Americans go to God and ask, "How long?" It is a worship that is connected to the real world and real problems that celebrates a God who is both transcendent and immanent. My momma would put it this way: "He is a God who sits high and looks low."

This God has manifested God's self throughout time, and African Americans look back at how God has called the African American church to be where we found that sweet resting place along with that peace that surpassed understanding. African American churches are connected to their history because they understand that God has revealed God's self through history, and they see their present ministry as an extension of the ministry of the ancestors and elders.

We will say more about what it means to be the African American church in chapter 3. However, we didn't want to make this next move in the book without at least giving a working definition of what we mean as we talk about being a part of the African American church tradition. As we move along in the conversation, we want to ask a series of questions with the ultimate goal being for us to act and become. As you read this book, please ask, What are the vital signs that determine if an African American church is dead or alive? As we pose this central question, look at your church and ask yourself, How would we answer these questions?

The Signs of Life or Death?

1. Is our worship a powerful experience that lifts people's spirits while preaching a liberative word? If so, how do we know? What qualitative and quantitative evaluative tools are we using to draw these conclusions?
2. Does our ministry profile reflect the ministry profile of Jesus as we see it in the Gospels according to Matthew, Mark, Luke, and John? Why or why not?
3. How diverse is our congregation in terms of age, gender, socioeconomic class, sexual orientation, and family type?
4. Are we experiencing sustained intentional numeric growth on an annual basis? Are we taking in new members who were previously unchurched in proportion to the population trends of our city? Why or why not?
5. Are we developing mature disciples of Jesus Christ by preaching, teaching, and serving the congregation and community? How do we know? How are we measuring?
6. How do our members acts as agents of outreach, making a positive difference in our city or community as active agents of liberation challenging unjust systems?
7. How much time do we spend in the community building relationships?
8. Are we developing partnerships with established community agencies? Why or why not?
9. How are we ministering to people as they navigate life's journey by having ministries that specifically speak to and with children, youth, young adults, adults, and seniors?

10. When new members join our community or church, how are we reaching out to them, welcoming them, and making sure they are integrated into the body?
11. How are we a distinctively African American worshipping community?
    a. How are we dealing with the struggles our people are facing in our community?
    b. What are we doing to make a real difference in the lives of African Americans?
    c. To what extent do our worship services reflect our culture? How?
    d. What are we preaching about? Are we dealing with issues of social concerns and liberation in our preaching?
    e. Is our praise and worship a vehicle by which those who worship with us feel that they have had an encounter with God during worship? If not, why?

Notes

1. Eddie Glaude Jr., "The Black Church Is Dead," http://www.huffingtonpost.com/eddie-glaude-jr-phd/the-black-church-is-dead_b_473815.html (accessed October 21, 2013).
2. Gayraud S. Wilmore, "Does the 'Black Church' Really Exist?" in *Africentric Approaches to Christian Ministry: Strengthening Urban Congregations in African American Communities*, ed. Ronald Peters and Marsha Haney (New York: University Press of America, 2006), 2.
3. Joseph L. White and Thomas A. Parham, *The Psychology of Blacks: An African-American Perspective* (Englewood Cliffs, NJ: Prentice Hall, 1990), 44.
4. James Cone, "What Does It Mean to Be Saved?" in *Preaching the Gospel*, ed. Henry J. Young (Philadelphia: Fortress, 1976), 21.
5. W. E. B. Du Bois, *The Souls of Black Folk* (1903; reprint ed., Millwood, NY: Kraus-Thomson Organization, 1985), 191.
6. Gilkes, Cheryl Townsend. *"If It Wasn't for the Women": Black Women's Experience and Womanist Culture in Church and Community* (Maryknoll, NY: Orbis Books, 2001), 6.
7. Gilkes, 6.
8. Wiggins, Daphne. *Righteous Content: Black Women's Perspectives of Church and Faith* (New York: New York University Press, 2005), 7.

2

Biblical Foundations for Future Ministry in the African American Church

Engaging Society as a Witness for Christ

JUSTIN G. WEST

In chapter 1, we laid a broad foundation of what we mean when we use the term "African American or black church" with some ways to measure if the African American church is alive or dead. In this chapter we want to continue that conversation by considering what it means to be a faithful witness of Christ in and to society. In subsequent chapters we will suggest that to be a faithful witness in and to society will require the church to become knowledgeable about some of the pressing issues and changes occurring in contemporary society. Before we explore the current issues of society, however, we should first explain why we believe the church must actively engage society as a witness for Christ.

Such an explanation for the church's participation in society as a witness for Christ is rooted in the Bible, which has served as the church's guide for mission and ministry throughout history. Therefore, this chapter will explore how God through the Scriptures places the call and responsibility on the church to witness to society through active participation, which includes responding to society's pressing concerns. Though the Holy Spirit has spoken to God's people throughout Scripture about their engagement with society, this section will lift up the mission and ministry of Jesus the Christ in the New Testament, as well as the mission Christ gave his disciples to carry out in the world.

We embark on this exploration with a question: What does the Bible suggest regarding the church's ministry? Believing that Scripture sheds light on how we should shape and develop our ministries, we affirm that God's people are called to be proactive witnesses in the midst of society. God's people are to have a presence and voice in society, which may require God's people to speak to the pressing concerns of society. As a part of God's people, then, the African American church receives the call and responsibility to be a courageous, attentive, and active witness in society, for society, for the glory of God.

Gospel Ministry: How Should We Do It?

We who make up the African American church comprise various backgrounds and traditions. Given this diversity among us, it is not unusual that some churches tend to emphasize parts of Scripture in their teaching that other churches do not, and vice versa. Although we have a common history as people in the United States, our churches have not and do not see eye to eye on all matters regarding Scripture. However, despite the differences between our Christian denominations, most of our churches would agree that part of what it means to be faithful witnesses of Jesus Christ is to proclaim the gospel to the world.

What is this gospel? Translated from the Greek, the word *gospel* means "good news." But when we examine Scripture closely, we see that the gospel is God's good news, and for several reasons. The gospel is the good news that God loved the world so greatly that the Father sent the Son, Jesus, into the world to save the world from perishing (John 1:14-18; 3:16-21); it is the good news that though we stray from God by sinning, God decided to embrace us with his love and offer us new life through Jesus Christ's death and resurrection (Romans 5:6-21); it is the good news that God will liberate us from all forms of oppression (Luke 14:4–16:19); and finally, it is good news because it gives us hope that death does not have the final word of our lives because God will raise us up to everlasting life (1 Corinthians 15).

This gospel is ultimately a matter of life or death, freedom or bondage, hope or despair, a life forever with God or a life forever without God. As persons who have come into contact with this gospel and experienced its transformative and liberative power, we should have a natural desire to spread this message to whomever we encounter. But more significantly, as disciples of Christ, we believe that Christ has given us a mandate to spread the gospel to the world—from our neighbors next door to our neighbors down the street to our neighbors across the oceans (Acts 1:6-8). We have an obligation to share the good news of Christ with anybody we encounter. As Christ says in a familiar passage (Matthew 28:18-20, NIV), "All authority in heaven and on earth has been given to me. Therefore go and make disciples of all nations, baptizing them in the name of the Father and of the Son and of the Holy Spirit, and teaching them to obey everything I have commanded you. And surely I am with you always, to the very end of the age." We know what we are called to do as Christians, as followers of Christ. We are called to proclaim the good news of the gospel. Scripture is clear about this.

But what is often more difficult for us to discern or deduce from Scripture is not always what we are called to do, but how we should do what we are called to do. In other words, how should we effectively spread the gospel to people of today, who live in a society so unlike the one in which the early disciples and Jesus lived? How should the African American church be the salt and light of the world (Matthew 5:13-16)? How should we be witnesses of Christ in the world today (Acts 1:8)?

These are challenging questions for us, especially when we consider the types of lives each of us lead compared with the lives of Jesus and the disciples. Our schedules are already full of things to do. From work to school to home to church to sleep to vacation, we don't seem to have the same amount of time that Jesus and the early church had to proclaim God's love to the world. Times have changed. And perhaps we think we don't have much time in our day to spread the gospel.

One answer, then, to the question of how we should spread the gospel message is that we need to find new methods to spread the gospel. The methods that people used at the time of the early church might not work for our era. Even having tent meetings in a field might not attract many persons today as they did just sixty years ago. Preaching by standing on a corner and using a megaphone might not strike people in the same way it did during evangelistic outreach in the 1970s. Successful methods for this century will most likely need to be new methods. So, what methods do we have to employ?

Despite the array of methods we may implement for communicating the gospel in our contemporary context (e.g., Facebook, Twitter, YouTube, movies, and other forms of multimedia and technology), there is another angle to answering "How should we spread the gospel?" that perhaps should draw our attention. Rather than exploring current communication methods, we should consider, first, what disposition toward society the church should take when proclaiming the gospel. In other words, before we talk about speaking or communicating the gospel, perhaps the church should examine its relationship with the larger society. For example, should the church share the gospel while alienating or distancing itself from society by staying fixed in our church buildings? Can we effectively share the gospel without being involved, concerned, and attentive to the issues affecting society?

When we consider Scripture, it seems that an essential piece to being effective witnesses (i.e., communicators of the gospel) begins with us being proactive agents in society. Instead of alienating ourselves or becoming passive members of society, Scripture seems to call us to become knowledgeable about the pressing issues that concern society. It advises that in order to reach people effectively, we must first know about those people. If people are to listen to and receive the gospel of Christ from us, we must first demonstrate to them that we care about their lives—the things that consume their time, the issues that move and inspire them, the issues that cause them pain or joy, and where they are most likely to spend their time.

When we examine the Scriptures, we see Jesus doing just this. He engages his society and shows concern for people who are suffering. In his ministry we observe a man who cares deeply for others and spreads the good news about God's reign while also setting aside time to listen to and address the needs of people. Only by entering into society to find out what was happening there was Jesus able to identify who needed healing for disease, who needed forgiveness, and who needed to hear the proclamation of the kingdom of God (Matthew 4:23; 9:25).

The important point for Jesus was not maintaining a certain social status by interacting only with certain people but approaching anybody with a need in order to help that person in his or her situation (John 5:1-14). In what many consider Jesus' first sermon, he outlines his mission: "The Spirit of the Lord is on me, because he has anointed me to proclaim good news to the poor. He has sent me to proclaim freedom for the prisoners and recovery of sight for the blind, to set the oppressed free, to proclaim the year of the Lord's favor" (Luke 4:18-19, NIV). In this statement, Jesus ties together action words that imply social engagement and proclamation. For Jesus, there seems to be no separation between preaching the gospel and practicing social activism, between speaking God's Word and enacting God's Word through social justice. Soon after this speech, in fact, we see Jesus engaging society by meeting tangible needs, as well as vocalizing the gospel (Luke 4:31-44). For Jesus, proclaiming God's good news, and specifically the kingdom of God, entailed that he embody this message by being knowledgeable, attentive, and responsive to the needs of the masses: "But if I drive out demons by the finger of God, then the kingdom of God has come upon you" (Luke 11:20, NIV). Jesus also makes this connection between engaging and meeting the needs of society and proclaiming God's Word when he instructs his disciples (Matthew 10; 28:16-18). In Luke 10:8-9 (NIV), for example, he tells them, "When you enter a town and are welcomed, eat what is offered to you. Heal the sick who are there and tell them, 'The kingdom of God has come near to you.'" Deeds and words—social activism and gospel proclamation—are held together.

Is such an engaged posture toward society alive in our African American churches? If we are to emulate Jesus, should not our gospel ministry be done as we engage our society around us—as we open our eyes to see, our ears to listen, our hearts to feel, and our minds and bodies to respond to the myriad needs that pervade our communities? It seems that to be proactive witnesses of Christ in and among society, we must be engaged in it. Certain church traditions might mean well to suggest that we must be separate from the world because of its dangers, or even that we must be in but not of the world, but our churches would do well to examine these statements against the backdrop of Jesus' and the disciples' ministry. Yes, Christians must be cautious of ungodly temptations of the world, but Jesus appears to operate not defensively but assertively, through his interacting with people and his preaching.

Although we've mentioned how interacting with society was central to Jesus' ministry, it might help to study one story that demonstrates the centrality. Let's look briefly at one that is familiar to many of us.

"This Man Welcomes Sinners": Jesus as Model

The heading above is taken from the beginning of the fifteenth chapter of Luke's Gospel and is the words of a group of Pharisees who, in that moment, are watching Jesus spend quality time with a group of so-called sinners. The words seem to indicate that the Pharisees are frustrated, aggravated, possibly very upset, because Jesus' actions surprise them. They do not expect Jesus to associate with sinners. They are confused about why Jesus is doing what he is doing. Though the text does not explicitly tell us the reason the Pharisees are frustrated with Jesus' actions—to the point that they mutter the above words—when we consider what has occurred so far in the book of Luke, we can gather some clues. We have only to turn to the previous chapter to get a sense of what the Pharisees might be thinking.

When we look at Luke 14, we notice another scene in which Pharisees are close to Jesus.[1] This time, however, it is the Pharisees, not sinners, with whom Jesus is interacting. In fact, the scene is the opposite of Luke 15. In Luke 15, Jesus is dining with sinners. In Luke 14, Jesus is having fellowship with Pharisees. In other words, Jesus has shifted his attention—he turns from Pharisees towards sinners. This shift in focus is perhaps the most striking part of the narrative, and it reasonable to suggest it is the cause of the Pharisees' irritation. Perhaps the Pharisees were thinking, "Why is this man, who spends time with us, now interacting with sinners?" To sense truly the depth of this situation, to grasp why the Pharisees are so disturbed, we must keep in mind the historical context of the text.

At that time in history, the Pharisees were known in society as a righteous people who knew the law and kept it. In fact, they kept the law so well that in Matthew's Gospel, Jesus says to his audience during his Sermon on the Mount that "unless your righteousness surpasses that of the Pharisees and the teachers of the law, you will certainly not enter the kingdom of heaven" (Matthew 5:20, NIV).

According to Jewish law, a part of being righteous meant that you had to hang out with the right crowd. You couldn't just hang out with anybody or everybody. To maintain your status as a righteous person meant associating with the right people, and the right people for righteous people were righteous people. Thus, being a righteous person meant avoiding people who were not considered righteous, and it meant, especially, not associating with sinners. If you hung out with sinners, you might have been perceived as a sinner or an unclean person and therefore lose your reputation as a righteous person.

This is the social expectation that the Pharisees had of people who ran in their circle. And this seems to be the expectation that they had of Jesus in Luke 15. How could a man who associated with them—righteous people!—now be hanging with unrighteous people? Furthermore, why in the world would he be eating with them? Joining anybody for a meal in those days was seen as an intimate, personal occasion. You didn't eat with just anybody. But perhaps even more significantly for Jews was the issue of purity. In Jewish culture, certain foods were considered clean or acceptable, and this food had to be prepared specific ways. Certain people were also considered unclean, because of their behavior (or physical conditions), and they most certainly would not have prepared clean food in the manner the Pharisees would have approved. This knowledge renders Jesus' sharing a meal with sinners that much more radical. Jesus is essentially communicating that including sinners is more important than adhering to the purity rituals.

This is where we observe the beauty and power of Jesus' actions, for in his turning from the Pharisees and his turning to sinners he reveals a striking image. He reveals that God chooses to deliver the gospel to sinners in society—to those the righteous looked down upon—not by remaining in the temple and preaching to those there, not by standing on a street corner and shouting the message through a megaphone, and not by marching down the street holding up a sign that condemns sinners. Instead, as Jesus welcomes and eats with sinners, he reveals the God who chooses to transcend the social and religious expectations to engage people in society who remained outside of the temple. In welcoming and dining with sinners, Jesus was performing public ministry that was concerned about addressing issues of the world around him. Jesus did not alienate himself from society or even persons in society whom leaders of his religion marginalized. His was no private religion. He was not limited to meeting the needs of faithful Jews who met at the temple. Rather, Jesus demonstrates a deep conviction to minister outside the church—and to do so by spending quality time listening and caring for the needs of the least of these and of society's marginalized. His was a public religion.

How Are We to Be Like Christ?

The question we should now ask is what Christ's ministry means for the church. Knowing the example that Christ set for his disciples, what should we now do in the twenty-first century as disciples who represent African American churches of a variety of traditions? As followers of Christ, as persons who have been called to seek ultimately to follow Christ, what does Christ's interaction with society mean for our ministries? Is Christ's ministry our model for ministry? If so, the model he sets for us is one that invites us, and even compels us, to be certain types of witnesses of his gospel in the world.

Jesus teaches us that ministry should not be done only in the religious sphere. Ministry cannot be done exclusively inside our churches or on church grounds or just among our congregations. On the contrary, ministry must be done in the public arena, in the places where "sinners" and those persons most ostracized by society are—on mountaintops and valleys, along the highways and subways and in other people's homes. Today, do we have a public religion, or do we limit the practice of our faith to so-called sacred spaces and to the privacy of our prayer closets?

The fact that Christ would sit down at the dining table with sinners is remarkable because of how society viewed hospitality at the time. By accepting an invitation to dinner, Jesus didn't just accept a free meal; he acknowledged the honor of sitting with those whom society called dishonorable. And because first-century hospitality consisted of a home-cooked, multicourse meal served over a period of hours, accepting an invitation to dinner meant a prolonged period of fellowship, talking and getting to know one another, even becoming friends. Sharing such a meal was considered a special occasion; when guests sat down at a host's table to dine together, it was an honor for all involved—and it was essentially an invitation to intimacy. There was a time for meaningful conversation to occur, about faith and family and politics and whatever else was on people's hearts and minds. It was a time where all parties could speak and all parties could listen.

The point of emphasizing the importance of eating at the table is to highlight the fact that by dining with sinners, Jesus was welcoming them—not only to sit in on his teachings but also to engage in his life, and he in theirs. Christ was not just saying "hi" to sinners and moving on. He was doing much, much more! He was spending quality time with them. He was listening closely and sincerely to their questions and concerns. Perhaps he was getting to know them on a personal level. Perhaps he was learning how they were raised, what kind of family they had, what struggles and pain they had experienced, and what types of things they enjoyed doing. And perhaps in the midst of their honest and transparent conversations, Christ had opportunities to share with them about his heavenly Father and God's reign.

In other parts of the Gospels, we observe that Jesus' ministry took place largely outside of the synagogues, and, unlike many religious leaders of his time, Jesus was trying to reach persons on the outskirts of the Jewish religious circle (John 4). In John 3–5, as well as in John 9, we see vivid examples of Jesus devoting his attention to the concerns of persons in his social space. In each of these chapters, John depicts Jesus as allocating time to have meaningful conversations with specific persons in his social world. In fact, in the story in John 4, Jesus has what at that time would have been a provocative interaction with a Samaritan woman. In this example, cultural and religious matters were involved that should have prevented Jesus from talking with this woman. Jesus was a Jew, and at the time, Jews and Samaritans had ethnic tension; it was commonly assumed that Jews and Samaritans avoided each other. But Jesus crosses this boundary. And he doesn't stop there.

Heightening the provocativeness of the situation further, Jesus crosses the established gender line. Women were viewed negatively, and their roles were confined mostly to domestic space. That Jesus interacts with the woman in public space was improper by those standards. Not only that, but a traditional belief was that especially Samaritan women were unclean from birth. Jesus' request of a drink of water from this woman meant he was entering unclean space, similar to his eating with sinners. But again Jesus cares more about the woman's needs than he does about propriety. He shows no fear in crossing the perceived social boundaries that we are often afraid to cross in our own time; he was more willing to take the risk of affecting a person's life by transcending social barriers than protecting himself from public contempt or ridicule.

With Whom Are We Dining?

Let's now turn to the church. If the church is to follow Christ's example and become effective ministers of the gospel, we must seek to initiate situations with persons outside our churches, showing them we care deeply about them. If we do not have a public ministry that welcomes persons in society—even those whom we consider to be "sinners" or outsiders—then how will we reach them? Why would they want to come into our churches to fellowship when we fail to show them that we care about them or their issues? As Christ models for his followers, the actions of spending time with people and getting acquainted with their issues may create a trust between those in the church and those outside of the church that will allow us to proclaim the gospel message to them more authentically.

When we recognize how Jesus did public ministry, we must ask ourselves a series of reflective questions about our ministries:

How can we do what Jesus did in our day-to-day lives?

How can we translate what Jesus did then to our ministries today?

How would it look for us to welcome and eat with "sinners" at our own dining tables?

How do we go to where people eat, sit, and talk so that we may connect with them and they connect with us?

Where do we go to listen to society? Where do we go to connect to society?

What walls must we tear down to free the church to be Christ's church and not "our" church?

How can we create space to welcome outsiders into our churches?

How can we show we care deeply for people and not just that we want them to come to our churches?

What social boundaries are we willing to cross for the sake of
Jesus Christ and his good news?

How are we alienating ourselves from the concerns of people
around us and what can we do to reverse this trend?

The questions listed above are meant to challenge us. Please,
don't take them lightly; don't brush over them, because they are
central as we focus on reviving, reforming, and resurrecting our
ministries in the image of God. We must all examine prayerfully
how we may be faithful to welcoming persons in our communities
who are not associated with our churches. What walls have we
established by word or deed that need deconstruction so that we
may welcome and eat with our neighbors?

For some churches, "welcoming and eating with sinners" may
mean having community picnics in the parks with our neighbors.
For other churches, it will mean having a food pantry giveaway
and hosting a meal with those coming to receive food so that we establish meaningful relationships with them. Other churches might
challenge their members to invite a person from work to their house
for a meal. For other churches, it might mean taking a group of
church members to a restaurant and inviting strangers who are sitting at other tables to our table to talk. It might just mean leaning
over to a person sitting at a table next to you at Starbucks and asking how that person is or showing some interest in what he or she
is doing. There may be many ways that we might implement Jesus'
model ministry in our own. But it will take prayer, thought, creativity, and courage to do something new, and maybe even dangerous.
Is the African American church willing to do this?

My hope is that we will begin to reflect on our ministries and ask
why they exist and why should they exist. The ministry of Christ,
as we have mentioned, occurred outside the walls of the temple.
It occurred on the streets as he interacted with everyday people,
some of whom were non-churched folk. But where do the majority
of our ministries take place? Do we have an outward focus? Have
we as the church focused too much on matters inside the church
to the extent that we have not engaged those persons outside of
the church? Have we become a church that serves its members and
teaches its members that ministry is member to member? Have we
become so concerned about maintaining our institutions that we

have neglected people who need to hear and be transformed by the good news of the gospel? Have we become so caught up in religiosity that we have forgotten that faith without works is dead (James 2:14-26)? Have we become so entrenched in worship services that we have ignored the fact that God desires justice instead of religious rituals (Isaiah 58)?

We cannot cast judgment on any particular churches or traditions in this respect, but perhaps we should all accept the challenge of asking these critical questions about our own ministries. Are we more inwardly focused than outwardly focused? What are we doing in our communities? Do the communities surrounding our church buildings even know that we exist? If people within our communities are not being influenced by us, if we are not ministering to them, then there might be something missing from our ministries. We might be too inwardly focused.

Let's turn back to Jesus. Jesus himself was concerned with a similar issue regarding the ministry of the religious leaders of his day (Luke 10). He was concerned that they were so focused on religious rituals that they were missing opportunities to serve those people outside those who showed up at the temple or synagogue on a regular basis.

For example, in the parable of the Good Samaritan, Jesus inserts two religious figures in the parable in order to illustrate a point about what it means to do ministry that involves loving one's neighbor. Jesus depicts a Levite and a priest who are traveling down a road on which a man who was beaten and robbed is lying, about to die. The situation is desperate for this man! If he does not receive immediate medical attention and care, he will certainly die. The man is bruised, bloodied, and hopeless. In a certain way, the setting is perfectly set for these religious leaders passing by to love and minister to this man. But as these religious leaders draw closer to this afflicted man, as they see the severity of his situation, they waste the opportunity. They don't help him. They pass by as if the man is not even there.

Let us use our holy imaginations for a minute and ask, "Why did these religious leaders pass by instead of assisting this brother in need?" We could suggest a couple of reasons. The religious leaders might have thought the man was dead, and to touch a dead man would have made them ritually unclean—unfit for leading religious services for the next week. (Even touching someone with open sores would have violated Levitical purity laws.) Alternatively, they might have been trying to get to the temple to take care of some religious matters, which they considered more important than showing compassion to a stranger. Whatever the reason might have been for these leaders, one thing seems clear in Jesus' parables: they did the wrong thing. They missed an opportunity to minister to the needs of someone in their society, to someone on their street, to someone right in front of their faces. We could probably say their ministry was too inward and not enough outward.

Even though this is a familiar parable to us, we should not overlook its profound message for our ministries. It requires us to confront several searching questions: Are our ministries focused on religious traditions and rituals to the extent that we fail to see opportunities to minister to persons outside of our churches' walls? Have we become so concerned with meeting our religious obligations that we are missing opportunities to show compassion and mercy to our neighbors next door or down the street? How can we regain the vision that ministry is more than catering to the needs of church folk? How can we reshape and recast our ministries in a way that they express love to non-churched folk?

This parable should make us think about who is that afflicted person in need of compassion that we pass by on the way to our church buildings. For me, the answer is right in front of me, just as it was for the Levite and the priest. On my way to church, I drive past Latino immigrants who stand on the corners on Sunday mornings waiting for work. The work line is long, and many of them might not be picked that day. The ones who are picked will work long hours for less than minimum-wage pay. Then, as I get closer to the church building, I drive past a Laundromat and see people who I imagine don't have the time or energy or money to do laundry during the week, pushing their heavy, overloaded carts full of clothes. As I get yet closer to the church building, I see people sitting in the park, looking tired and having conversation, and I ponder what they could be struggling with.

I wonder why they are not at church, I wonder if the church has ever tried to help them, and I wonder how the church can help them. And sometimes I can't help but think that I am going to the wrong place. On the basis of religious tradition I shouldn't be going to a building dressed in a suit. I should be in a tee-shirt and jeans, conversing with the people I am passing by and sharing with them the good news of God. That might be where the church should be sometimes—in a park talking to strangers, listening to their concerns and needs and responding in love through intervention, be it physical, financial, or other types of support, as did the Samaritan in the parable. Perhaps they need a hand pushing their laundry. Perhaps they need advocates to stand up for them so they can earn decent wages.

Jesus often reminded the religious leaders of their need to look beyond religious ritual and personal piety to matters of more importance. In fact, in one instance Jesus comments on the tithing of the religious leaders. He informs them that they are becoming so consumed by paying tithes that they are missing out on more important issues. What he tells the Pharisees is that tithing has not just become a religious obligation. It has become something that they value more than justice, mercy, and faithfulness. And so Jesus calls them out on this very matter: "Woe to you, teachers of the law and Pharisees, you hypocrites! You give a tenth of your spices—mint, dill and cumin. But you have neglected the more important matters of the law—justice, mercy and faithfulness. You should have practiced the latter, without neglecting the former" (Matthew 23:23, NIV). When Jesus warns the Pharisees and religious leaders about their actions, he was not saying that everything they were doing was wrong. Likewise, we must not think that everything we are doing in ministry is wrong. This is not the point. Jesus was not condemning them because they were tithing. No, what he was calling them out on was that they were missing a more important part of the law: practicing justice, mercy, and faithfulness. In other words, it seems that the Pharisees placed more value on what they were doing inside of their religious circle than on what they were doing to meet people's needs in society.

While many of us are doing some great things in our ministries, we must continue asking ourselves if we need to refocus and reflect on what we have left undone. Are we emphasizing something in ministry that is less important than caring for the needs of people? Are we emphasizing coming to church on Sundays or to Bible studies rather than encouraging our members to be activists in society doing justice and acts of mercy? Again, there is nothing wrong with going to church and Bible studies. But there might be something wrong when attending these services becomes more important to our faith than spending time helping meet the urgent needs of our neighbors. Are we putting so much of an emphasis on tithing in our worship services that we neglect to remind our people that when they begin their week they should look for opportunities to show mercy to their neighbors and remain faithful to their God?

A Concluding Word

Ministry entails service. Therefore, to minister to people involves serving those people. The questions we raised in this chapter are, How do our church's acts of service look? What is our model for ministry? As the body of Christ, we suggest that to be Christ to the world, we must elevate Christ's life as our model for ministry. We must seek to emulate the way Christ lived, which first begins by studying Christ. When we do so, we recognize several distinct features about Jesus' ministry that should influence and shape how we do ministry.

First, Jesus was not preoccupied with spending his time ministering only to religious people, but rather he sought to serve people whom religious people despised (Luke 5:29-31; 15). Jesus welcomed and ate with sinners. Jesus cared for people who had been ostracized because they had a certain diseases or physical afflictions (Matthew 4:23-25; 8:1-4; Mark 10:46-52; John 5:1-8). People who spent time in the religious establishment at the time were confused and startled by Jesus' actions, for he did not do what was safe or expected of him (John 4).

Second, Jesus focused his ministry on meeting the needs of people who were politically, economically, and socially oppressed or marginalized; as Jesus declares about his own ministry, "The Spirit of the Lord is on me, because he has anointed me to proclaim good news to the poor. He has sent me to proclaim freedom for the prisoners and recovery of sight for the blind, to set the oppressed free, to proclaim the year of the Lord's favor" (Luke 4:18-19, NIV).

Third, Jesus proclaimed the kingdom of God, but his teachings were connected to his acts of service in society (Matthew 4:23; 9:35). As Jesus reached out to people, he proclaimed the good news of the kingdom.

Questions

1. How do we attempt to follow Jesus' example in our ministries?
2. How are we proclaiming God's Word to society while meeting the needs of society?
3. How are we serving the least, the lost, and the lonely?
4. Where do we need to go and what do we need to do to be more like Jesus?
5. How are we leaving the building to be the church?
6. Who aren't we reaching?
7. Who are we passing on the way to church?
8. What do we need to do less of?
9. What do we need to do more of?
10. What do we need to stop doing?
11. What do we need to start doing?
12. As we reflect on the ministry of Jesus Christ, where do we come up short?

Notes

1. We assume that the Pharisees in Luke 15 might be some of the same Pharisees in Luke 14 and earlier in the book of Luke. Luke does not indicate this, but we believe the text leaves us with the freedom to interpret it either way. From our perspective, that they were the same Pharisees seems to fit better with the structure and coherency of the text, as explained by our interpretation. In other words, the Pharisees mutter because the man who had been associating with them—righteous people—was not "lawfully" supposed to interact with sinners or unrighteous people.

3

Sankofa Spirituality[1]

Looking Back While Looking Forward

RALPH BASUI WATKINS

We want to continue to push the question, What does it mean to be an alive African American church? We continue to push this question because we believe it is at the heart of our conversation. Chapter 2 began a conversation around some of the biblical foundations for mission of the church, and this chapter extends that conversation by looking back at how the African American church or congregations have lived that mission. As we look back at the roots of our tradition, it is our hope that this will serve as a foundation for our future. In this chapter we are called to remember so that we will not forget. To remember has to be an intentional act. We don't remember automatically. We can forget more than we remember if we aren't intentional about remembering. If we don't remember we become dis-membered, disconnected from the source of our identity, and the result is we don't know who we are.

When our adult children come to visit my wife and me, we tell old stories and look at old pictures and videos in an effort to remember. We are intentionally memory making. We do the work of remembering so that we don't forget. To remember is a part of our identity construction. The African American church must remember. If we don't remember, we will be held hostage to an identity that is rooted only in the present with no appreciation for its roots. A church without roots is a church that will go with the wind of the day and have a fragmented identity. It will be a church with nothing to hold onto. By contrast, when a church understands its history and knows who it has been, then it can carefully and intentionally negotiate its relationship with its present and future in relationship to its past. To remember is not to be held hostage to the past, but it is to recognize that you are to be connected to that past. The African American church of today, in all of its diversity, is a child of its history. To honor that history is to know it by remembering and then asking, How do we grow out of our history?

My First Sankofa Moment: If It Wasn't for the Women

Cheryl Townsend Gilkes put it this way: "'If it wasn't for the women,' the black community would not have had the churches and other organizations that have fostered the psychic and material survival of individuals and that have mobilized the constituencies that have produced change and progress."[2] Gilkes couldn't be more right. African American women have sustained the church and developed this theologian.

When I think of my history with the church, I think of my earliest Sunday school teachers; they were women. I can see Mrs. Ruby Thomas at St. Lawrence African Methodist Episcopal Church in Eatonville, Florida, encouraging me to ask questions, teaching me to think theologically. Nurtured by women in the context of the church, my earliest theological reflection occurred. And what stuck with me was those women's understanding of God—what I later learned to name a womanist understanding of what Kelly Brown Douglas calls the Black Christ.

A womanist understanding of the Black Christ is, at core, seeing Christ in the faces and witness of the women who have led African American churches. These women embodied the Christ they taught about. They were Christ for me in their witness and helped me challenge the biological construct of the Messiah. They showed me that it was Christ's actions more than Christ's gender that made Jesus the Messiah. According to Kelly Brown Douglas, from a womanist perspective, this Black Christ says three things I want us to consider:

First, it says that the Black Christ is present in the Black community wherever people are engaged in a struggle for that community's "wholeness." Second, it challenges Black people to participate in activities that advance the unity and freedom of their community. It allows them to know Christ is with them and in them anytime they promote life and wholeness for Black men and women. Third, to portray Christ in the face of Black heroines and heroes signals that it was not who Jesus was, particularly as a male, that made him Christ, but what he did.[3]

The Black Christ from a womanist perspective calls me to recognize the witness and power of the women who saved my life and who have saved the black church. It calls us to embrace the three dimensions of a liberative womanist witness that Douglas teases out in her work. As we embark on this Sankofa moment, let us look back to our churches, to the pews, the ushers, the Mother's Board, the kitchen, the missionaries, the Sunday school, and what do we see? I see women as the Black Christ setting our people and me free. At the core, these women were salvific black love. They gave themselves to a loving, liberative God and to God's church. We must give ourselves to this same type of love if we hope to be alive black churches. "To give ourselves love, to love blackness, is to restore the true meaning of freedom, hope, and possibility in all our lives."[4]

The Root and the Fruit

If we don't know from whence we have come, we don't understand who we were and how that history might help us define who we are to be as the African American church. As we explore this historical conversation, we encourage you to review your congregational history, your denominational history, and the larger history of the African American Christian religious experience. Although each congregation and denomination is unique, the African American Christian religious experience is cut from a large tree with common branches. (See the end of this chapter for recommended history books that might serve you as you continue this conversation.)

I have found as a pastor that many people in my congregation weren't as familiar with our roots in the context of our Christian tradition and denomination as I would have liked for them to be. Other times, congregations can get caught up in the history of the church and its tradition, particularly in worship, but they weren't informed as to how we got these traditions. The traditions became the thing that was worshipped at the expense of the larger liberative tradition that gave birth to what we did in worship. (More on this in chapter 5.)

When we review our history, we see at the root that our tradition was one that freed us to become a new and liberative expression of what we had protested against. The forming of the African American Christian church was a protest against the white Anglo-Saxon Protestant tradition. The European Protestant tradition was a protest against the abuses of the Catholic church, and the birth of the African American Christian tradition was a protest against the racist roots of the European American Protestant church. This prophetic protest, which asserts the right to be a free church, is at the root of our tradition.

If we don't embrace the roots of our tradition, then the question becomes, Are we truly a part of that tradition? The major issue here is identity and mission. Who are we, and what cloth were we cut from? What should that cloth look like today? Let us look back, not with romantic rose-colored glasses but with an eye for connections. How are we connected to this historical legacy we call the African American church, and how do we express this heritage today? We are not called to be who we were yesterday, but we are to be an extension and new creation of that older tradition today. If we don't know our history or if we are disconnected from that history, we will miss the direction the past can provide us in the present.

To Serve the Present Age:
From the Past to the Present and into the Future

We are co-creators with God as God shapes the church for the future. It is important that as we, with God, shape that future, we look back to those times when God was using the church in a liberative way. When our models for ministry are all contemporary models, we miss what came before them. If these contemporary models have no historical foundations, we cannot be sure about from whom and from whence they have come. They have no roots. When our contemporary models of church are ahistorical and we embrace them as models of ministry, we too can become ahistorical. When you are ahistorical, you are rootless, which means you lack a strong foundation to steady you when the winds of change and challenge blow. A healthy engagement with your history is an important guide for your future.

When we talk about the African American church from a historical perspective, we have to consider its roots in this strange land in America. In 1971 Rev. Otis Moss Jr. gave us six broad distinctives that relate to the historic roots of the African American church. These distinctives are worthy of being considered today. They will serve as an outline to guide our conversation about the historical foundations of the African American Christian religious experience:

1. The black church is the church of the oppressed, and the white church is the church of the oppressor.
2. The practicing religion of the black church is generally a theology of survival. It is also a carrier of the black folk culture. The practicing religion of the white church, with certain exceptions, has been American culture and racism. Ours is a theology of hope.
3. The black church has been distinguished greatly by a dynamic and free pulpit. . . . The black preacher is primarily concerned with whether God will approve.
4. The black church provided integrity (and gave a sense of self-worth to its people).
5. The black church also provided for social unity. It has provided a social house, a culture center, a freedom house. It has provided limited educational support. It has provided a meaningful spiritual legacy. The thrust for freedom by black Americans found a home in the black church.
6. The black church converted oppression into poetry, exploitation into creative force, humiliation into a hunger for justice, haunting fear into hymns of faith. If this church is to remain relevant, it must convert a praying people into a positive power-conscious people. Prayer must find fulfillment in revolutionary action. Remember that prayer without action is empty. Remember also that action without prayer is dangerous.[5]

The Root of Freedom Fighting

When we look at the first distinctive as laid out by Dr. Moss, it is the foundation of the church being a church that is about liberation. It is a church that was born out of oppressive conditions, and those conditions, as they related to the trajectory of expressions along racial lines, were about white over black and our church fighting against racial oppression. Is this distinctive still relevant? That question would be answered by another question: Is racism still operative in our society? If the answer is yes, that racism is still operative in our society, then a call to the African American church would still be to fight against racism, if that church claims to be a black church that is linked to its historic foundation.

While there have been gains by celebrated African Americans, the overwhelming majority of our people are still the victims of a system that is fed by systemic racial discrimination. In chapter 7 we shall talk about the top ten social issues facing African Americans, so we will not ponder this point here. Suffice it to say that the evidence is clear, even in a post–Obama America, that African Americans are still oppressed along racial and class lines. The very foundation of the African American church was to speak to this oppressive condition in two ways. The church spoke to African Americans by telling us that we have a sense of agency. We are called to act as proactive agents for our liberation. Liberation begins when you free yourself to construct a sense of self and to think about freedom. The act to think free is the first act of freedom. Africans were taught to love their God and themselves enough to act on that love, and the act of fighting for liberation was a loving act. Just as God stepped into history in the person of Jesus to act as an agent of liberation, so too are we to act as agents of liberation, and that first act was how we saw ourselves as children of God.

The second act of liberation was lived out as the African American church called the white power structure to task. The founding mothers and fathers of this rich tradition didn't back down from the oppressors. They called those oppressors what they were as they looked them in the face and told them that acts of racist oppression were contrary to the ways and Word of God. Evidence of what we are arguing is evident in the founding of the African Methodist Episcopal Church in 1787. Bishop Richard Allen, the leader of the Free African Society, was clear as he and his band of followers refused to be demeaned by the whites at St. George's Methodist Church.

> Richard Allen did not believe in insults and his blood literally
> boiled when told to go to the gallery of St. George's Church, and

when told to move again in the midst of prayer his cup ran over. In this very act Allen's view of the dignity of man [and woman] is clearly demonstrated. He just could not and would not endure discriminatory practices based upon color.[6]

Richard Allen, along with other men and women of color who had been subjected to racial discrimination, saw fit to shake the dust off of their feet and birth the first African American denomination. At the foundation of their quest was the search for freedom: "For African Americans freedom has always been communal in nature. In Africa the destiny of the individual was linked to that of the tribe or the community in an intensely interconnected security system."[7] It was not enough for Allen and his followers to set up an independent congregation. They saw their plight and the future of liberation as linked with their brothers and sisters who to were subjected to racial discrimination in America. At the core of the Free African Aid Society was to work to free other Africans who were enslaved. You had free Africans working to free enslaved Africans. This connective tissue of liberation is in the DNA of the African American church.

If you move from the African Methodists to the African American Baptists, you see shared roots. As the African American Baptists made their decision to form their own denomination free from the oppressive forces, "there were two principal factors which led ultimately to the exodus of black Baptists from white churches. One was the segregational and discriminatory policy of most white Baptists. The other may be expressed as the new theological awakening among black Baptist preachers."[8]

While there was a theological awakening among black Baptists, at the root of their formation of their own denomination was their concise decision to say no to the racism they were subjected to in their relationship with the white Baptist power structure. This move for independence, similar to that of the African Methodists, was not limited to a congregational freedom. Rather, these leaders were thinking of freedom on a grander scale. They saw fit to develop a denomination with a structure to support other congregations and individuals in their quest for freedom. At the birth canal of the African American religious experience is this quest for freedom.

C. Eric Lincoln and Lawrence H. Mamiya put it this way: "Unlike most sectarian movements, the initial impetus for black spiritual and ecclesiastical independence was not grounded in religious doctrine or polity, but in the offensiveness of racial segregation in the churches and the alarming inconsistences between the teachings and expressions of the faith."[9] Even African American churches that are labeled nondenominational have roots in these historic expressions of black faith. The religious roots of such congregations go deep into the personal histories of the founding pastor and individual members. Consider: What are their historical denominational roots? What are their African American religious roots? When we trace these roots they can become sources to our future. When we claim our roots, we see how we were connected, are connected, and should be connected to our past. There should be no African American church that doesn't have some expressed lived connection to its historical liberative roots.

A Theology of Hope

When we say a theology of hope, we are not thinking of the German theologian Jürgen Moltman, but rather we are thinking of the African American preachers and lay leaders who believed in a God who would come through. They believed in a God who could and would make a way out of no way. This theology of hope is what could more accurately be labeled black theology.

According to Will Coleman,

> Black theology is a theology of witness and liberation . . . it attempts to discern and proclaim God's presence in liberating those who suffer under the various forms of sin and oppression. These oppressions include racism, sexism, classism, and imperialism. . . . Black theology [focuses] upon analysis, interpretation, and proclamation of how God liberates African Americans (and other oppressed people) from oppression.[10]

A black theology of hope is a theology that proclaims God's presence in the midst of suffering, while pointing to how God is acting as an agent of liberation. It addresses the right-now while pointing to tomorrow. We have hope because we know a brighter day is coming. We know that God is working.

Black theology points to a God and the acts of God in real time, in real ways, doing things through the body of Christ that are making a difference in the day-to-day struggles of African American people. When we study social movements that have led to systemic change in American culture, we see the connection between a freedom movement, big picture, and small picture in how this movement affected the everyday lives of people. For example, as much as the Montgomery bus boycott was a social movement, it also directly affected the everyday lives of the people. The mass meetings and Sunday worship services were living witness of a black theology of hope. African American churches reach back and reclaim this message of hope and live out a liberative ministry that gives our people a reason to shout.

Preach, Preacher: A Free Pulpit

The African American preacher's voice is to be the voice of God on behalf of the people. He or she speaks for us; they are the ones we have invested in. We have supported their training and called them back home to serve. As God called Moses to speak to Pharaoh, so God calls the African American preacher to speak liberative truth to oppressive power structures and those who lead them. She or he is to be that free voice because God and the church have your back. While others in our community may be reliant on an employer, the preacher is employed by God and supported via the church, in part or in whole. The expectation then is for the voice of the preacher to be uninhibited. The preacher has tenure with God, and his or her call cannot be revoked. When we say the preacher is that free voice we are suggesting that the preacher can afford to speak truth to power on behalf of the people because the people are one of the pastor's sources of financial and spiritual support. Preachers have been trained to dissect unjust structures, bring them to light, and walk with the people as they seek to establish a more just world.

The free pulpit is one of the fountains of life for the African American church and community. African American preachers in historical context didn't just speak on behalf of their congregation but rather for the community as a whole. The African American preacher has been in touch and in tune with the community. The connection the African American preacher has with the broader community empowers him or her with the heart, hurt, and pain of the African American community. When he or she stands and says, "The people say," we are in real solidarity.

Preachers shouldn't speak *for* the community; rather, they should speak *with* the community. They should know the people who are experiencing the struggles of which they speak. They should be in touch, literally in touch, via deep relationship with those individuals who are experiencing the oppression that the preacher speaks against. Preachers who lead do so out of relationship with those whom they march with, sit with, protest with, and ultimately fight with against oppression, side by side. Preachers who hope to be a part of this tradition of being that free voice from our pulpits will have to make sure they nurture their relationship with the larger African American community that is diverse in so many ways.

African American preachers are active participants in the life of the African American community because they seek to have that relationship. Traditionally, African American preachers have not driven into the church parking lot, gotten out of their car, preached, returned to their car, and left the neighborhood. They have been organically connected to the community, which makes them one with their congregation and those who live around the church. The free pulpit in the African American tradition has been a product of the incarnational relationship the preacher has had with the masses of the people.

For the African American tradition the only way to be free is to be connected. Freedom struggle is rooted in relationship. Although we live in an age where the class divide is more pronounced in the African American community than in ages past, the preacher should find creative ways to reconnect with the masses. This may mean that we have to make a special effort to build those relationships with the community that surrounds the church. We can't be a part of a struggle that we don't know. We can't lead a people whom we don't love. We can't love a people whom we don't know. If we don't know the people by being in living relationship with them, then we are at best in a fragmented relationship. Incarnational ministry requires that we come and are one with the people. We are the people, and the people are us. We have to remember that we are in this thing together.

We Are the Body of Christ: We Serve with Integrity

When Richard Allen led that small band of faithful out of St. George's Church in Philadelphia in 1787 and went down the road and established Bethel African Methodist Episcopal Church, he felt he was establishing true Methodism. Allen wasn't starting a radical group of believers; rather, his intent was to be true to what he understood it meant to be the church of Jesus Christ. At the root of the African American Christian identity is this issue of integrity, of being true to what it means to be the church. The African American church at its inception took ecclesiology seriously. The integrity of what it means to be the church of Jesus Christ, as modeled in the ministry of Jesus Christ while he was here on earth, is the milk upon which the African American church was grown.

How do we reflect on the ministry of Jesus and its core principles as a guide or foundation of how we live out our ministry today? This is what I am pushing us toward. The model of ministry I see in Jesus is one that was about service and liberation, and it happened on the ground. Jesus went to be with the people and meet their needs. Jesus didn't complain about the masses and their hunger, but rather he saw to it that they were fed. Jesus spoke against institutions that didn't respond to the pain and hurts of people as he responded. He taught us to do the same.

Models of ministry come and go, and they have the potential to be the fad of the day. The African American church is not to be a church of fads, or trying to put into to place the latest marketing strategy that attracts the most members. The key here is integrity. As we look at the ministry of Jesus and the foundations from Scripture that inform what it means to be the church, we hold true to those things. Those principled truths from Scripture are the guides to our desire to hear from God, "Well done, my good and faithful servant." When I think of the principled truth in Jesus meeting the woman at the well (John 4), we see a Jesus who was more concerned about her need for both physical and spiritual water even when those around him asked why he was talking to her. We are called to embrace the principled truths of talking to those the world has put aside. We are called to be a part of that prophetic tradition that birthed our faith, which was not a faith that stood at one with the empire but looked on the empire with disdain and objection. The church lived a ministry that not only sided with the oppressed, as Luke 4:18 suggests, but also came to set the oppressed free.

Unity in the Community: Different Denominations, Same God, Same Aims

The motto of the Universal Negro Improvement Association (UNIA) was "One God, One Aim, One Destiny." Although the UNIA, started by Marcus Garvey in the 1920s, was not a church, its motto symbolizes the role the UNIA, along with the black church, played during that time in history. Congregations, denominations, and civic organizations such as the UNIA and the National Association for the Advancement of Colored People (NAACP) may have seen the means to freedom differently, but they all would agree that the God they served is a God who was about their freedom. (The rich heritage of the UNIA and the NAACP, both born in the early 1900s, was a public expression of African Americans' yearning for freedom. These are two of our historic freedom organizations that were supported heavily by the church. These are organizations worthy of your research when time permits.) Similarly, while congregations and denominations have differences in doctrine, as branches grafted to the True Vine they served as institutions that brought people together. They were the center of community that served as the catalyst for community building. This effort of community building extended across denominational lines and local geographic lines.

To be true to this heritage, we have to seek to be that place that brings people together. The African American church is to be intentional about community building. To build a community means we attend to the building blocks of a community. The building blocks of communities are families, cross-generational supervision (adults knowing each other and watching out for one another's children), quality public schools, civic organizations, recreation centers, religious centers, political engagement, and a strong socioeconomic structure that in turn produces a strong infrastructure and safe community that sees itself connected. Unity across African American denominations is possible when we share that common bond of historically being that social network and cohesion for the African American community.

The Transforming Power of the Church: From Blues to Gospel

How do we deal with the pain index of the continuing oppression, discrimination, and tax of being black in America? Do we preach "you are next in line for a blessing" or "enlarge my territory"? Do we preach "it will all be better by and by"? Do we preach "hold on, a change is coming"? What do we preach, and how do we address the blues of life with the good news of the gospel of Jesus Christ?

Historically the African American church has wrestled with this question. The preaching wasn't shaped to tickle the ear, but rather it was framed to analyze those forces that mitigated against living a full life and then provided biblically informed strategies to transform a system that produced inequality. In our musical expressions, the message from blues to gospel was as much about your personal problems as it was about how liberation was to come to the community. It wasn't merely about *your* breakthrough but also about *our* breakout. In our cultural religious expressions as in our music, we have experienced collective blues and we have lived a communal gospel. The good news is that God loved the world, and this included us, and God sent the Son to set us free. The gospel as preached and lived deals with the blues the people are facing. The gospel is that good news in word and deed that addresses the blues and helps people find a new life and a new song.

Our conclusion? If we are to call ourselves the African American church, we must have a sense of our roots. We must know that we are branches in a well-developed vineyard. This vineyard has some good fruit and some bad. Some of the branches need to be pruned because they are dead or diseased, but the root is still good. Be encouraged, claim your roots, and allow God to lead you as you water and grow the next branch of this great tradition. We are a part of that True Vine, and we are the branches as God calls us to reach out to lift up to make this world a place where the love and liberative presence of God is recognizable as God's church serves as an instrument of liberation.

Questions

1. What are your congregational roots in the historic African American church?
2. As you look at the distinctives that were outlined in this chapter, how are these distinctives alive in your congregation?
3. What do you claim from our history that needs to be further developed in your ministry today?
4. How is your congregation distinctively an African American church?
5. How do you wear your blackness inside and outside the church?

Notes

1. Sankofa is an Akan word (a language of Ghana) that means, roughly, "to reach back and get it." It is often associated with the African proverb, "It is not wrong to go back for that which you have forgotten."

2. Gilkes, Cheryl Townsend. *"If It Wasn't for the Women": Black Women's Experience and Womanist Culture in Church and Community* (Maryknoll, NY: Orbis Books, 2001), 7.

3. Douglas, Kelly Brown. *The Black Christ* (Maryknoll, NY: Orbis Books, 1994), 108.

4. hooks, bell. *Salvation: Black People and Love* (New York: William Morrow, 2001), xxiv.

5. Adapted from Otis Moss Jr., "Black Church Distinctives," in *Black Church Life-Style: Rediscovering the Black Christian Experience*, ed. Emmanuel L. McCall (Nashville: Broadman, 1986), 14–17.

6. Howard D. Gregg, *History of the African Methodist Episcopal Church: The Black Church in Action* (Nashville: AMEC Sunday School Union, 1980), 27.

7. C. Eric Lincoln and Lawrence H. Mamiya, *The Black Church in the African American Experience* (Durham: Duke University Press, 1990), 5.

8. Leroy Fitts, *A History of Black Baptists* (Nashville: Broadman, 1985), 43.

9. Lincoln and Mamiya, 47.

10. Will Coleman, *Tribal Talk: Black Theology, Hermeneutics, and African American Ways of "Telling Story"* (University Park: Pennsylvania State University Press, 2000), 171.

Recommended Reading

Alexander, Estrelda. *Black Fire: One Hundred Years of African American Pentecostalism*. Downers Grove, IL: IVP Academic Press, 2011.

Battle, Michael. *The Black Church in America: African American Christian Spirituality*. Malden, MA: Blackwell, 2006.

Dallam, Marie W. *Daddy Grace: A Celebrity Preacher and His House of Prayer*. New York: NYU Press, 2009.

Fitts, Leroy. *A History of Black Baptists*. Nashville: Broadman, 1985.

Gregg, Howard D. *History of the African Methodist Episcopal (A.M.E.) Church*. Nashville: AMEC Sunday School Union, 1980.

Lakey, Othal Hawthorne. *History of the CME Church*. Memphis: CME Publishing, 1996.

Lincoln, C. Eric, and Lawrence H. Mamiya. *The Black Church in the African American Experience*. Durham: Duke University Press, 1990.

McMickle, Marvin A., ed. *The Encyclopedia of African American Christian Heritage*. Valley Forge, PA: Judson Press, 2002.

Robeck, Cecil M., Jr. *The Azusa Street Mission and Revival: The Birth of the Global Pentecostal Movement*. Nashville: Thomas Nelson, 2006.

Townsend, Cheryl Gilkes. *If It Wasn't for the Women: Black Women's Experience and Womanist Culture in the Church and Community*. Maryknoll, NY: Orbis, 2001.

Walls, Jacob William. *The African Methodist Episcopal Zion Church: Reality of the Black Church*. Charlotte: AME Zion Publishing House, 1974.

Wilmore, Gayraud S. *Black and Presbyterian: The Heritage and the Hope*. Louisville: Witherspoon Press, 2006.

4

Models of the African American Church in Conversation

JUSTIN G. WEST

This chapter examines how various models of the African American church may benefit from interacting with one another. It explores how praise churches and prophetic churches can learn from each other's unique gifts—how what shines in prophetic churches can help illumine what is dim in praise churches, and vice versa. For example, while prophetic churches may teach praise churches that being a faithful witness of Christ in society includes engaging the political and social issues of the day, praise churches may remind prophetic churches that the problems African Americans face in society are not merely physical problems but spiritual problems that require God's people to receive spiritual nourishment through meaningful worship experiences on Sunday morning in order to engage the spiritual dimension of such problems. For this reason, these traditions of the African American church *must* have an open conversation.

What's more, we will consider how other models of church, including future models and models that have often been left out of the conversation, might assist the African American church in being an effective witness in society. We will ask what models of church can benefit both praise and prophetic churches. In addition, we will briefly explore how church models outside of the African American church might strengthen it. Finally, this chapter will also examine how various black experiences, especially those of younger generations, call for the African American church to be open and willing to change so that it may incorporate multiple models of church. Such changes may result in the church becoming an even more effective witness for Christ and his gospel in the world.

In chapter 3, we surveyed the history of African American churches and suggested that, based on this history, several features mark African American churches collectively. (Revisit the six elements listed in chapter 3.) African American churches share these features because African Americans have a common history of encountering and opposing racism as a people living in the United States. Highlighting these common features across the national landscape provides a way in which to speak of these congregations as a united African American church. However, even though throughout our history as African Americans in the United States we have shared certain lived experiences and certain religious movements, differences between African American Protestant churches have made it difficult to speak as the African American church as one, united entity; in fact, at times there have been vast differences between churches.[1] In this chapter, we invite readers to consider a few key differences in popular trends in African American churches.

For various reasons—from interpretation of Scripture to regional influences to varying emphases on worship practices—African Americans have established churches in denominations that we still see today: Baptists, Methodists, Church of God in Christ (COGIC), Pentecostals and neo-Pentecostals, and more. What we see in the history of Christianity among Africans in America is that as more Africans appropriated the Christian faith, certain groups of Africans adapted the faith to fit their present situation. Consequently, an array of denominations developed, taking distinctive forms, often emphasizing specific religious practices and doctrines over others in their churches. For example, while some African American churches incorporated doctrines, creeds, and worship practices from Anglo and other European denominations into their congregations (sometimes adapting those practices as well), other churches retained and transformed particular aspects of African religious practices, connecting them to a "Christian" way of life, and some churches found themselves in between and outside of these trends.

Growing Connectedly Apart

What emerged from the late nineteenth and early twentieth century was a tremendous expanse of the African American church. By the middle of the twentieth century, the spatial growth of the African American church took a distinct shape as Africans migrated from a declining agricultural economy in the South to a booming industrial economy in the North. However, at the same time that African American churches grew numerically and spatially during those periods, settling down in various regions, the churches did not always grow together or establish intimacy among themselves. Rather, because of theological and spiritual differences existing among the denominations, a social gap developed between them. In other words, the result of some churches' stringent adherence to specific forms of spirituality was a choice not to associate with churches which did not adhere to the same forms.

A startling statement by Albert Raboteau describes in part the social divide that characterized the relationship between such churches: "Social critics have complained that the proliferation of black churches fragmented the black community into competing sects. If only they had overcome their differences, the argument goes, black churches might have pooled their resources and become an effective force for the economic and social development of the black community."[2]

That church affiliation had a role in dividing black communities rather than in uniting and strengthening them may show just how separated African American churches were at that point. But why was this? Were the churches so unlike each other that in addition to being unwilling to work together they were also unwilling to listen to and learn from each other? As we consider this history, let's also take a look at the present state of our churches, as well as the future. Do these divisions among our churches continue to exist? And if so, what would happen if, rather than churches continuing to allow the gap between them to expand, they began to close it? What effect would this have on our communities, on society at large, and on individual African Americans still struggling against oppression in the twenty-first century?

Locating Praise and Prophetic Churches

Despite denominational affiliation, each local congregation in the African American church has distinguishing features. Whether the church identifies as Methodist, Baptist, Pentecostal, independent, or nondenominational, a church's social environment, leaders, and demographics of the members influence how that local church functions—each taking on distinct characteristics. Nonetheless, while it is obvious that such denominational and demographic diversity exists among congregations, there are at least two clear ends of the African American continuum that describe the functionality of the African American churches: the praise and the prophetic.[3] Although many churches fall somewhere between the two extremes of the continuum by having some mix of prophetic and praise characteristics, our aim here is to deal specifically with those churches that gravitate more toward one extreme and intentionally or unintentionally neglect the other. As we examine each side of the same branch, I hope to offer a snapshot of why most of us will tend to categorize specific congregations as praise versus prophetic churches and why a local church might lean more in one direction over the other.

I invite you to also join me in thinking of what congregations that are inclined to praise or prophetic might receive if they proactively engaged the other side. What wisdom would they receive? How might they be edified? How might the African American church as a whole become a more unified body and perhaps that "effective force" that Raboteau described—a force that ministers to the range of needs among people both inside and outside the church? As we explore each side of the continuum, praise and prophetic, it might help us to be conscious of the areas of our ministries that could learn from churches of other traditions.

Gravitating Toward Praise

When we use the term "praise" to denote specific churches, we are not suggesting that these churches are being characterized as such based on the amount or form in which they praise God; instead, we use the term to capture the emphasis that a church places on its actions inside a worship setting. This emphasis is mostly embodied in a Sunday morning service, in contrast to a church in the prophetic tradition, which emphasizes its actions outside of worship, in the community and public arena. Thus, for our purposes in this book, describing a church as a praise church is simply a way to articulate the main qualities of the church. Such a designation should not be interpreted to mean that all of African American churches falling more into the praise category are absent of any notion of the prophetic; likewise, don't conclude that all congregations oriented toward the prophetic don't have praise qualities. We merely use these terms to circumscribe churches whose distinctive features fit into our descriptions below.

Centered in Worship

That said, there a number of features that we believe characterize praise churches. The most significant characteristic is that they are churches that orient their ministries inward. They have a focus on ministering to the spiritual needs of their members and the persons within the church doors. Their main concern is to sense the spiritual needs of the congregation and to connect them to God in such a way that those needs are met.

Although there are several ways in which praise churches may attempt to connect their people to God, their efforts—their preparation, training, and investment of resources—to make this connection usually culminate in how they function in worship gatherings on Sunday mornings. It is within the context of worship that the life of praise churches is most on display. In other words, praise congregations tend to focus significantly on connecting people to God through worship: by song, testimony, Scripture reading, and the preached Word. For this reason, these churches are usually recognized by their harmonious and well-trained choirs, their captivating and charismatic preachers, and their spontaneous and emotive worship expressed through song, dance, and shout.

As Dr. Watkins alluded to in the introduction, an example of such a church would be The City of Refuge in Covina, California, where Bishop Noel Jones is pastor. But a megachurch like City of Refuge is not representative of all praise churches; rather, there are many types of praise churches that range in size, location, and denomination.

For example, I have experienced praise churches in a Baptist tradition of two hundred members, as well as in rural congregations that struggle to get seventy-five people present for a service.

Pentecostal Roots

Many praise churches have their roots in the holiness-Pentecostal movement, a church movement that has a rich history of innovative worship experiences dating back to the turn of the twentieth century. Many of these churches incorporated certain African religious practices (such as the ring-shout) into their worship, which took shape in the forms of drum beating, loud singing, and ecstatic dancing, all becoming significant marks of their spiritual life together.[4] From the early twentieth century until now, the music of Pentecostal churches has been a benchmark of their worship experience, and that music has laid the groundwork for such musical movements as gospel music.[5]

Gradually, Pentecostal churches received the reputation for being great places to worship. It is widely known among African American churches, for example, that if you step into a typical Church of God in Christ congregation, you are going to encounter a high-energy, free-flowing, spontaneous worship experience that is rich in singing, dancing, and shouting. Matching the energy level of the music is, of course, the preaching, which is also typically engaging.

Biblical Foundations

Most praise churches have good reason for focusing their ministry on Sunday morning worship. They claim solid biblical precedent for their decision. Consider the scriptural passages that exhort the people of God to praise and worship through gathering together to sing, shout, make music with instruments, and proclaim God's Word. Among these passages are many of the psalms. For instance, Psalm 147 (NRSV) begins, "Praise the LORD! How good it is to sing praises to our God; for he is gracious, and a song of praise is fitting." Psalm 150 has almost become a creedal basis for the type of worship in praise churches: "Praise the LORD . . . Praise him with trumpet sound; praise him with lute and harp! . . . with tambourine and dance . . . with strings and pipe . . . with clanging cymbals . . . with loud clashing cymbals! Let everything that breathes praise the LORD! Praise the LORD!" (Psalm 150:1,3-6, NRSV). Passages such as these give biblical foundations to how many praise churches function.

Surviving Reality

Another basis for this internal focus on worship is historical and social, for in many ways the worship experience in praise churches on Sunday mornings has been an experience that has worked to help African Americans survive the realities of racism and oppression that they have faced throughout the week. This is why, for instance, Gayraud Wilmore has labeled these churches as being of the "survival tradition."[6] Some persons who stand outside praise traditions have been critical of their limited (or nonexistent) social and political engagement, but we should also recognize the ways that worship in these churches has galvanized and strengthened many African Americans, enabling them to make it one day at a time against society's odds.

Wilmore highlights this important aspect of praise churches when he says, "This survival motif is closely associated with authentic African American religion in its *alternating phases of withdrawal* from and the aggressive opposition toward the white world."[7] Lawrence H. Mamiya and C. Eric Lincoln seem to describe a similar thing when they use the label "priestly tradition."[8] Lincoln and Mamiya elaborate that the priestly function of black churches—in contrast to the prophetic function—entails that they "are bastions of survival" for black folks. In other words, despite their lack of social or political activism, black churches of this "survival tradition" have had a central role in helping blacks to survive despite dire conditions of oppression because of the hope, faith, and encouragement they have experienced within the churches' walls.

Liberating Praise

Another way to understand the uniqueness of praise congregations is to view their worship as a form of liberation. Unlike other forms of liberation (for example, political, social, or economic), liberation in worship happens through the collective power of the sermon, the music, and the atmosphere of the churches. One understanding of liberation is that it cannot occur until social, political, and economic evils cease, but another understanding of liberation is that, although it lies in the future, it can break into our present situations. It can be a mystical experience that we have in a single moment when we encounter God and consequently release our concerns, worries, and fears in God's presence.

Theologian James Cone explains how we might experience liberation in the present: "Liberation as a future event is not simply *other* worldly but is the divine future that breaks into their social existence, bestowing wholeness in the present situation of pain and suffering and enabling black people to know that the existing state of oppression contradicts their real humanity as defined by God's future."[9] In the worship experience of praise churches, liberation may come in a psychological, emotional, or eschatological sense as people are reminded of the hope, the goodness, and the justice they believe is in God.

A Critical View

For some African Americans, the significance of praise churches is often overlooked. Some people are quick to disdain praise churches for being wildly behaving, irrational, and emotionally stimulating churches that lack theological substance. Other critics characterize the atmosphere as an opiate for the masses, momentarily dulling their senses to or distracting them from the issues they should be addressing in society. Some critique praise churches for having a preoccupation with praise and worship, lacking a preached prophetic Word, and overemphasizing individual spirituality and financial prosperity. Still others view some praise churches as overly concerned with form and style during worship, accusing such congregations of "performing" in their music or preaching, with more interest in "entertaining the audience" than in discipling or convicting the people of God.

Although these critiques can become overgeneralized caricatures that don't accurately represent many churches in the praise tradition, there is also sufficient validity in the observations to warrant legitimate attention and real reform. We will examine these issues later in considering what the praise tradition has to learn from the prophetic tradition.

That said, we believe that critiquing praise churches without attempting to learn what is powerful about them (i.e., why people attend them) can result in an oversimplification of the experience within praise churches and miss the value of the experience altogether.

Learning from Praise Churches

So, what might the African American church at large learn from the tradition of praise churches? First, many praise churches remind us that what happens in the worship space on Sunday significantly affects a person's life. As Dr. Carolyn Gordon, one of my preaching professors at Fuller Theological Seminary, suggested in a course on African American preaching, "When people go to church on Sunday, they are in a life-and-death situation." In other words, what they come to experience on Sunday has the capacity to give life or to offer death.

What Dr. Gordon was suggesting to the seminarians and future pastors who sat listening attentively to her wisdom was that people who come to church on Sundays could be on the verge of giving up on God and giving up on life. They come to worship on Sundays needing an experience that will inject just enough life into them to help them "keep on keeping on." To put it another way, praise churches remind us that when people come to church, they expect and need to have an encounter with God; they expect to receive a hope-filled vision of how the world will be, not a constant drilling about how it is and how they need to fix it; and they expect to get a foretaste of the world to come and of the celebration that we will hold when we gather around the throne to worship the Lamb.

In *Name It and Claim It*, Stephanie Mitchem asserts that because of the history of African Americans in society, African Americans have had a spirituality of longing—a longing for safe places where a person can encounter God.[10] Mitchem explains how some churches have met that longing by providing people with a worship space in which to belong and to feel secure. This is what many praise churches do well. They create this space and allow people to enter into it—if only for a few hours, get filled up, and leave with an encouraging, hopeful vision of the world that God intended and will eventually bring to reality. In sum, as Lincoln and Mamiya state, praise churches have been black churches "in search of transcendence, not a mere emptying of the emotions, but an enduring fellowship with God in which the formal worship service provided the occasion for particular periods of intimacy."[11]

But while praise churches offer experiences that some of our churches can learn from, we have already noted that one thing that some do not always do so well is to engage concretely the social, economic, and political injustices of the day. Rather, their battle is often fought in spiritual realms through the praise, worship, and prayer that occur in the safe enclosures of their own buildings. It is here that praise churches should heed the messages and activities of prophetic churches. Let us now examine what a prophetic church is and what it does well.

Gravitating Toward the Prophetic

The congregations of African Americans that fall on the side of the prophetic have a keen and critical eye for the injustices occurring against African Americans in society and take practical steps to confront these injustices and transform society in the process. They do not consider it enough for a church to confront life's hardships and society's injustices only through prayer or to escape them temporarily in enthralling worship services on Sundays. Rather, these congregations realize that many injustices are communal problems that require their church communities to partner with one another and other social organizations, pool their resources, and proactively, with hands-on activity, resolve.

They are churches that care equally (or more) about what is happening outside the walls of the church in comparison with what is happening inside the walls. This is not to say that prophetic churches do not have powerful praise and worship experiences, but many of them are known less for their preaching and music and more for the way they work to help persons in their community who are unsure of where the next job will come from or how they will pay their bills, fearing whether or not they will get a warm meal tonight, or worrying about their health because of lack of medical coverage.

Prophetic churches might care less about you walking away from a worship service feeling great inside and more about you becoming inspired and challenged to serve victimized and exploited persons in society. Furthermore, their pastors are not afraid to speak boldly from the pulpit about the social, economic, and political sin that is causing injustices in the community. Their pastors will boldly condemn institutional and systematic racism and other forms of oppression in society no matter the cost, and they are not afraid to challenge publicly their congregations to become involved in transforming society into a more just place.[12]

Prophetic churches are more inclined to view God in Christ as liberator of the oppressed, in contrast with praise churches' tendency to emphasize Jesus as personal Savior. Prophetic churches are more likely to appropriate the theological perspective that black theologians and womanist theologians have articulated since the late 1960s and early 1970s: that to be on God's side means to strive proactively to liberate oppressed persons from social bondage.

Biblical Foundations

When it comes to the Bible, prophetic churches will emphasize themes in Scripture that call for God's people to be attentive to the concerns of marginalized persons and advocate on their behalf. Prophetic churches are churches that believe the gospel calls them to be on the front lines of society, attempting to make change and to bring about justice. For prophetic churches, passages such as Luke 4:16-21 and Matthew 25:31-46 do not get spiritualized or allegorized; Jesus was really concerned about caring deeply for the prisoners, the physically ill, the orphan and the widow, and all those whom society might consider the least or the weak. Prophetic churches would hold that because Jesus "stood in the prophetic tradition when he taught what criteria would be used to judge the nations—it would not be through observance of narrowly defined religious duties but by whether they fed the hungry, clothed the naked, visited the sick and imprisoned."[13] They must also stand in that tradition.

As the influential black theologian Dwight Hopkins remarked about such churches,

They provide preaching that uplifts people's souls but also moves their spirits to go out to change the material world as they confront groups with disproportionate privileges and harmful powers. . . . Prophetic churches preaching and practicing black theology offer healing for the black family and make available therapy sessions, marital counseling and conferences, prison visitations, drug counseling, domestic violence ministries, support for lesbian and gays, and networking among professional blacks so that they can do pro bono work with working-class members of the church and broader communities.[14]

In other words, churches inclined toward the prophetic are organizing programs and social initiatives that seek to meet the many needs of people who experience any type of marginalization in society, be it because of race, class, gender, or sexual orientation.

Though there are many churches that exemplify the prophetic, one of note is Trinity United Church of Christ, based on the south side of Chicago. For years, this has been a church whose voice and actions have epitomized what it has meant to side with the oppressed in society. Even as this book was being written, they were planning to combat the ecological injustice that plagues urban environments by creating gardens for which neighbors will have the responsibility of planting, caring for, and harvesting their own fresh produce.

In contrast with praise churches, in which personal liberation might take place in the midst of powerful singing and preaching, prophetic churches are concerned about other forms of social liberation. They are concerned about fighting in a more public arena for economic, political, judicial, and ecological liberation, which for them is connected to spiritual liberation. They work toward poor people experiencing freedom from the crippling chains of poverty. They fight for the freedom of the many colored bodies which remain unjustly incarcerated and separated from themselves, their families, and the world. They work actively in politics to change educational policies that would make equal funding and quality teachers and curriculum available for public schools where ethnic minorities have a dominant presence. They speak against political figures who want to cut funding for programs that assist the lower classes and who easily spend more money making war around the world.

A Critical View

But just as some praise churches receive critique, prophetic churches have certain tendencies that also warrant critique and attention. For example, although many prophetic churches orient themselves to be involved in social justice in society, some of them may not recognize the importance that Sunday worship has for an individual's life. Although prophetic churches rightly exhort their members to be active agents in society to remedy injustices that attack communities, some may do so at the expense of missing the priestly function of churches, which is to minister and care for the individuals who step through their doors.

Where prophetic congregations fall short in this area, they might do well to learn from what some of their brothers and sisters in the praise churches are doing. But the key for both praise and prophetic churches to learn from the other is establishing dialogue between them.

Holding Conversation

In mapping out the distinguishing characteristics of praise and prophetic churches, I hope that I have presented how these types of churches could learn from each other. In fact, I would like to suggest they *need* each other. As a local church benefits from the gifts that its individual members offer, so too the larger church benefits when local churches offer their unique gifts and strengths to one another.

However, realizing that one church is not complete in itself and that it can learn from another church is not a position that one can typically arrive at easily or without sacrifices. In fact, some may even be put off by such a suggestion. "You mean to tell me *that* church can offer something to us? Oh, no . . ." I can already hear the complaints and see the defensive postures that some might take to such a suggestion. "No, not *that* church. Not *that* pastor. Our pastor has a vision from God, and we should just follow that." Some churches may feel comfortable with their own individuality and mission and may view working with other churches as either unnecessary or a daunting task.[15] So, what are practical steps our churches can take to initiating dialogue?

Perhaps a first step might be to consider the similarities churches of either tradition have with churches "across the road." And there may be no greater or powerful similarity than the fact that they profess to worship the same God, the God who called us into ministry in the first place, the same God whom we believe loves all and wills that all receive God's love. Although differences exist in interpreting and applying some texts in Scripture, is there no text that speaks of God that our churches embrace and that should bring us together? Steps can be taken, if churches are willing, to find ways to have a conversation with churches in their communities that are unlike their own about their similarities.

Building Bridges

When conversation is established between churches, the next question is how churches can begin to work together, to do ministry together, to serve their community together, to worship together, to learn and grow together. This is an important question to address, and the answer may be different for various churches and communities. Regardless of a church's social environment, we can suggest a few ways that churches might begin to address that question.

One place to start is with the pastors. For many African American churches, the pastor will play a vital role in helping churches connect to each other. As the shepherd of the church, the pastor must demonstrate by his or her leadership the importance of churches coming together to serve and to learn. Although pastors from different churches will not agree on everything, if they can at least have transparent conversation with each other, they might find ways that their churches can unite in the church's mission.

Another area to build bridges is through sharing in worship experiences. What if churches in your community were intentional about coming together for worship at least once per month? What if choirs and pastors rotated at these services to give all the churches in attendance a different perspective of worship and a different angle on Scripture? How might this setting offer churches on the praise or prophetic side a broader vision of worship and ministry?

Finally, a third suggestion for building bridges between praise churches and prophetic churches is to partner in efforts to serve the community. Can churches commit to pooling resources, sharing leadership, and setting aside a time to work together to be witnesses of the gospel? Can churches join hands in giving to the poor among us, marching for justice in their communities, and spreading the gospel to people who haven't received it? Perhaps these are questions that can be answered only after churches first learn to talk with each other and worship together. But they are still questions that churches from either side can begin thinking about even before dialogue starts.

Where Do We Go from Here?

To return to our initial assertion, "praise" and "prophetic" are only suggestive labels that are intended to get us to think about how a large number of congregations in the African American church tradition function. Absent from much of our conversation, however, is consideration of how other churches function—churches that don't fit neatly within either of these categories or that lie in the middle of the two extremes. Still other churches consider themselves historically African American churches but look very different from the majority of African American congregations. Furthermore, we haven't addressed what should or could happen as members of the younger generations, which develop in a society that looks very different from the past, will want to shape their local African American churches.

Changes, of course, are imminent. So, how will the church universal and local address them? For example, there is a movement among younger generations called Emerging Black Churches, which, like their Anglo counterparts, are tired of meaningless, irrelevant traditions and practices and are boldly rethinking these practices and traditions, hoping to bring change. But the overarching challenge that these minority churches within the black church pose is not unlike the work that praise and prophetic churches must do among each other. That is, how can the congregations that have a dominant presence among African American churches learn from churches in the margins and emerging churches of tomorrow's generations?

Questions

1. On what end of the continuum of African American churches would you locate your local church?

2. In what areas of your church's ministry are you partnering with other churches in your community? How do you think local churches can partner more than they do now?

3. In what ways do you think partnership in gospel ministry with other churches can change and transform your community?

4. How often do you worship in a church that is different from your own tradition? What might you learn if you did this more often?

Notes

1. See C. Eric Lincoln and Lawrence H. Mamiya, *The Black Church in the African American Experience* (Durham, NC: Duke University Press, 1990). This book offers a more thorough account of the history that contributed to this.

2. Albert Raboteau, *A Fire in the Bones: Reflections of African-American Religious History* (Boston: Beacon Press, 1995), 108.

3. See Michael Battle, *The Black Church in America: African American Spirituality* (Malden, MA: Blackwell, 2009). Battle does an admirable job of differentiating forms of the black church. He shows how, contrary to the popular notion that there is a distinguishing feature representative of all black churches, the black church has always had diversity among its various church bodies.

4. Cheryl Sanders, *Saints in Exile* (New York: Oxford University Press, 1996), 63–64.

5. Lincoln and Mamiya, 361–64.

6. Gayraud S. Wilmore, *Black Religion and Black Radicalism* (Maryknoll, NY: Orbis, 1998), 255–60.

7. Wilmore, 260.

8. Lincoln and Mamiya, 12.

9. James Cone, *God of the Oppressed* (Maryknoll, NY: Orbis, 1997), 146.

10. Stephanie Mitchem, *Name It and Claim It* (Cleveland: Pilgrim Press, 2007), 30.

11. Lincoln and Mamiya, 6.

12. Lincoln and Mamiya, 12.

13. Desmond Tutu, *God Is Not a Christian* (New York: Harper One, 2011), 162.

14. Dwight N. Hopkins, *Head and Heart: Black Theology—Past, Present, and Future* (New York: Palgrave, 2002), 20.

15. I'm reminded of a provoking conversation Barack Obama has with a Rev. Phillips on the south side of Chicago as Obama requests help from churches for his community organization. At the end of the conversation, when Obama is about to leave, he comments, "If we could bring just fifty churches together, we might be able to reverse some of the trends you've been talking about." But Rev. Phillips, who

knows well the difficulty of bringing divided churches together, responds informatively, "You may be right, Mr. Obama. . . . But you see, the churches around here are used to doing things their own way. Sometimes the congregations even more than the pastors." Barack Obama, *Dreams from My Father* (New York: Three Rivers Press, 2004), 274.

5

How to Reach and Keep What You Got

RALPH BASUI WATKINS

This book calls for a revival of the African American church and for outreach to the younger generation, but there is a tension in this call. In this chapter we put squarely on the table the challenges of developing new life, when attracting new members often produces a new congregation. As a church grows younger, how do its leaders deal with the balance of power in leadership between the elders and young adults? This chapter is meant to give your congregation the license to have a conversation about change and help you navigate this thorny terrain of becoming.

Change is difficult, and the older we get the more we tend to be resistant to change. I have reached that over-fifty mark in my life, and I am more set in my ways than ever. Congregations are like people; the older they get, the more they become set in their ways. The more mature and established a congregation becomes, the more tradition has a way of defining that congregation. To challenge or change those established traditions is a difficult thing for long-standing congregations to accept, and members and leaders alike tend to resist changing or altering those traditions.

This chapter identifies the key issues in the change process and puts on the table the key questions that congregations must ask: What is it that God is calling us to be in this present age? Are we willing to have the difficult conversations and to walk in the inevitable tensions of change? As the local church seeks to be faithful and serve in the twenty-first century, how should we change what we do? If the world has gone through a fundamental shift via current technology, how does this reality inform how we do what we do? How are we church in an age of Facebook, Instagram, and YouTube, when the device that keeps people connected is the cellphone and not the church bulletin? How does the church revamp itself to connect and serve in the present age while not forgetting the age from which it was birthed?

Yes, people will get angry and threaten to leave, and some will leave. They will pull out membership certificates, birth certificates, denominational identity, and church résumés as a way to assert their authority and to claim that they have a right to define the future direction of the congregation. These tactics of power are often rooted in fear and a struggle for security that is a part of this highly uncertain redefinition process.

In the end the questions we must continually return to are, What is God calling us to be in this age? What does God want for us as a congregation? As we think about engaging in this conversation about change while being true to our past, here are some initial questions to get the conversation started:

Who are we really as a congregation? Not what our church motto or mission statement says, but who are we really?

How would we describe our church?

How would a visitor describe our church?

How would a young adult child, niece, or nephew describe our church?

Do we want to grow? (Remember growth means change; radical growth means radical change.)

Do we want be a different church ten years from now? Why or why not?

How much change are we willing to initiate and sustain?

What are we not willing to change? Why?

What is not on the table? Why?

When we look at what is not on the table, the question becomes, why *isn't* it on the table? Do we have a biblically principled rationale for not having it on the table?

What are our obstacles to growth and change?

What are the traditions that served us well in the past that don't serve us well in the present age?

What comes first—our Christian identity and Scripture or our denominational identity?

Are we Baptists (insert your denomination) who are Christian or are we Christians who are Baptist (insert your denomination)?

How am I going be an active supportive participant in the process?

Maybe I should save such questions for the end of the chapter. That's the typical format for this kind of book. However, I believe we can use these questions as a lens through which we engage this chapter.

When I was a young preacher, it was a given in my underdeveloped mind that all churches wanted to grow. To be assigned to a church as a pastor and get up to preach that first sermon and see empty pews bothered me. It bothered me because I knew that there was someone who could benefit from being a member of this faith community and that this community would benefit from their presence. I thought those empty pews bothered everybody. Most members would agree with me in meetings that they wanted our church to grow, and they, like me, wanted the church to be full. What I came to find out was that they wanted the church to grow, but they didn't want the church to change.

When a church grows, it becomes a different church. You can't grow and remain the same. Growth demands change—change in leadership, change in how we do things, change in who is involved in decision making, change in how we relate to the pastor, and the list goes on and on. If we aren't willing to change, we are essentially saying no to growth and no to becoming the church that God would have us become.

Congregations, like people, become complacent and comfortable with the status quo. We become comfortable and secure in our relationships and traditions. We are used to the way things are and the way we do things. To be invited to grow is an invitation to change. It is an invitation to be uncomfortable. It is an invitation to live in tension. If a congregation isn't willing to be uncomfortable and disturbed, then it doesn't want to grow. If we aren't willing to be uncomfortable and live in tension while becoming what God would have us become, then we will die a slow death as our old ways become our death nail! In other words, to grow, we must purposefully alter our routines and approaches. As George Barna points out, "the Bible is equally clear in telling us that God did not send Jesus to die so we might be comfortable and complacent, but so we might die to self, pick up our cross, and follow the way of the Master."[1]

Tradition(s): Good and Bad

The source of our comfort comes in the form of our traditions. Don't get worried; I am not going to suggest you throw all of your traditions out the window. Traditions are needed, and they have the potential to give form, shape, and substance to a community. The question in this context is, Are the traditions we are holding onto doing what they once did? Is there a way to analyze our traditions so that we can discern the difference between those we need to hold onto, those we need to modify, and those we need to retire? Is there a way to talk about our traditions not being that which defines us? "That is what makes us _____." Fill in the blank with your denominational identity or church name. "That is what makes us First Baptist." "This is what distinguishes us as AME."

What are our roots? Are we rooted in our tradition or in our biblical mandate to be the church of Jesus Christ? Is it the call to worship that makes us AME, or is it our being connected to the liberative tradition of Jesus and the work of Bishop Richard Allen and Sarah Allen? Bishop Allen didn't birth the African Methodist Episcopal Church around a call to worship but a call to liberate Africans. So, should we be talking about our mission or our order of worship?

When it comes to the historic traditions in the church, we have to confront the fact that most of the things we are holding onto aren't biblical. In *Pagan Christianity?: Exploring the Roots of Our Church Practices*, Frank Viola and George Barna argue:

> The practices of the first-century church were the natural and spontaneous expression of divine life that indwelt the early Christians. And those practices were solidly grounded in the timeless principles and teachings of the New Testament. By contrast, a great number of the practices in many contemporary churches are in conflict with those biblical principles and teachings. When we dig deeper, we are compelled to ask: Where did the practices

of the contemporary church come from? The answer is disturbing: Most of them were borrowed from pagan culture.[2]

In essence, what Viola and Barna are saying is that most of what we do isn't biblical, so why argue over changing it? Many of the traditions we celebrate in the church have been borrowed from the larger culture in an effort to connect with the culture and the people. For example, the wearing of robes is linked to academia; in an attempt to look more scholarly and connect with those who were learned, the clergy donned the robe. Choirs singing in the choir loft is borrowed from the world of theater, where the performance of music was rooted; that performance model was brought into the church to connect with those who were accustomed to listening to music in that form. Dressing up for church is borrowed from the world of business and has no biblical foundation.

As shocking as Viola and Barna's title may be, the juxtaposition of the terms "pagan" and "Christianity" suggests that many things we do in the church aren't rooted in Scripture but rather are rooted in the culture. Thus, a great deal of what the church does could be considered "pagan." That label doesn't make something bad, but it points to how we have attempted to connect the gospel with a people and a culture at a given point in history. If we look at what we are doing today, we can then ask, Is it biblical? If the answer is no, then we can inquire of its roots. If those roots are cultural and were developed for a time when we were trying to connect people with the gospel, we can then ask what things we might consider to help us reach people in this age that is rooted in our love for God and our love for others.

Therefore, as we look at our traditions and consider how we engage them for this age, we need to go back to Scripture as a principled document to inform why we do what we do. As we establish the why of what we have been doing, we are empowered then to ask, How do we do what we do today, in this age?

For example, why do we have devotions to begin our worship service? It could be a time that we pause to recognize the presence of God and prepare for worship. It could be a time to share concerns and provide space for lay leaders to participate in the pre-worship and worship experience. We could even argue that, historically, devotion has been that time of settling and focusing the people. The question becomes, What form should devotion take in this era?

Should it look like it always has or should it be different? What are the biblical and cultural roots to our devotion period? Why do we have devotion? What is its purpose and function, and is it accomplishing that purpose? When we answer the why, we can then go on to ask, What should devotions look like in this age? Should we move from deacons leading hymns to a praise team or some other form of centering? Should we have moments of silence, meditation, prayer? The point here is simple: The why should inform the what and the how.

Consider other examples, these illustrating even more clearly the cultural (pagan!) origins of our traditions. It is a historical fact that preaching from the pulpit, processing in, sitting in pews, wearing usher uniforms, preparing Sunday bulletins or programs, and donning choir robes are not biblical mandates. I don't want to digress into deconstructing the roots of each of these practices (Viola and Barna do that in their book), but I do want to highlight these and many other traditions. These practices were brought into the church from the larger culture in an effort to connect with the world. They aren't bad in and of themselves, but if they are the basis of our identity as a church, we may be falling into a type of idolatry.

The point I am trying to make is that the things we argue over most aren't rooted in Scripture, the document that should guide our lives together. We need to investigate the roots of our traditions, and what we will find is that most of what we do isn't biblical, no matter how functional and mission-minded it may have been in ages past. Therefore, we need to ask, How do we accomplish those same goals today, with practices that are related to former traditions but aren't restrained by past or present traditions?

The church has always used things from the "pagan" culture to connect the Christian faith with the people in our world; the problem is that we have a tendency to forget why we adopted those practices in the first place (or even that the practices were adopted). The challenge in this age is the same as it has ever been: to update the things we use from the present culture to connect with people in the present age. (The unique part of this generation's challenge is that, because change in the world is accelerating so rapidly, it is difficult to keep up, much less to filter which innovations will be around long enough to integrate into the life and practice of our faith community.) We have to be wise about what we adopt, and love must be our guide. We must care enough to change in order to reach those we aren't reaching, while retaining enough of our historic identity to keep those with whom we have walked over the years. This doesn't mean we adopt things that are immoral or merely expedient, but it does mean we have to change if we hope to share the love of Christ in a changing world.

Scripture should guide us, along with our congregational and denominational history. Our history shows us how we have used a variety of innovations (concrete, behavioral, and ideological) from the culture in the context of congregational life to connect with the world. Bottom line: we are going to have change some stuff. In an age where people are connected via their gadgets, we can't expect the sign in front of the church to be the key means of sharing what the church is doing on a weekly basis. People are going to Google your church before they visit your worship service. A church that has no Web presence is a church that doesn't exist for many people. In an age where people are fast becoming visual learners, our teaching will have to include visual images to support our message. We are going to have to change how we communicate to the world outside the church.

Don't misunderstand me. I'm not suggesting that those who celebrate tradition and defend it are somehow demonic. Our traditions have served us well, and they speak to who we are and were. I love to wear a robe and stand in the pulpit and preach in such a way that my words are flowery and poetic. The question for me is, How do we respect the robe and the preaching, as an example, and then ask, What should preaching look like in this age? How do we preach to a visual culture that is more casual? Do I dispense with the robe and flowery language? Do I use screens and projectors to make points and tell stories? Do I start to use video clips to introduce my sermons? And, what should the content of sermons be in this age? Do I need to get back to basics of the Old Testament stories and Jesus' teachings, instead of assuming an audience raised in the Sunday school felt bored? In an age of the nones and the spiritual-but-not-religious, do I need to ask more questions and equip people to navigate a wider range of answers? We have to rethink not only how we preach but also what we preach.

The things I am suggesting come from the culture. Will these changes, from one tradition to establishing a new tradition, fundamentally alter who we are as a church? Yes—and no! I am still preaching, but I am preaching in a way that those who have heard and those whom I want to hear can hear. Our worship music may sound different. We may be singing praise songs instead of hymns, but we are still worshipping the same God. We may have praise teams instead of mass choirs, but we are still worshipping the same God. Things will sound and look different, but at our core we remain a church that is rooted in Scripture while seeking to connect in an age that has changed. At our core, we are the same Bible-believing church, and as we radiate from that core, we live out being church in radical new ways and expressions that put us in touch with the world.

We have to engage the roots of our traditions as they were originally established—in conversation with Scripture and the larger culture. This is not easy. It is hard to decide what to hold onto and what to let go of, and that is why we have to do both. We have to hold on *and* let go. This is a tension we will have to learn to live in, as we live in a time of transition. This is hard work! Congregations must be willing to do this hard work and have these very difficult conversations. There is no way around it. We have to keep that key question in mind: What is it that God would have us to become? And then, How will our commitment to sharing the love of God, to attracting, inviting, and adopting new members into the family of faith, make us faithful to God's call to make disciples?

Holding On and Letting Go for the Greater Good

We are in the midst of a cultural revolution. People are no longer coming to church because "I was raised in the church" or because "This is my family's church." Young adults today "have no use for churches that play religious games, where those games are worship services that drone on without the presence of God or ministry programs that bear no spiritual fruit."[3] People want to find God and be part of something bigger than them. While we hold onto our historic identity, there must be room for what people are looking for—and they are looking for God. When we look back at the historic foundation of our faith traditions, we find at its root the same thing people are looking for today: God. When the dust settles, we find God and we find people trying to connect with God. As the church, we have to make sure we are connected to God and the gospel of Jesus Christ as the center of who we are and what we do.

What do we hold onto? We have to hold onto the gospel of Jesus Christ. In some instances, we may have to recover the gospel. That idea may be hard to address, but we have to put the question on the table: Is the gospel of Jesus Christ our guide, or is it our Book of Order, Book of Discipline, or our church bylaws? Have our bylaws made the gospel bygone?

Author Gabe Lyons put it this way in *The Next Christians: How a New Generation Is Restoring the Faith*:

> The first thing for Christians is to *recover the Gospel*—to re-learn and fall in love again with that historic, beautiful, redemptive, faithful, demanding, reconciling, all powerful, restorative, atoning, grace-abounding, soul-quenching, spiritually fulfilling good news of God's love. . . . Following Jesus in the twenty-first century demands that God's disciples relearn the full meaning of the Gospel story.[4]

This may sound trite, but I argue that it is profound and liberating, as we embrace the love of God as a love that was so powerful that God was willing to give God's Son on the cross. The love of God is so powerful that God watched Jesus die on the cross.

When we embrace God's love, what are we *not* willing to change for the sake of this love? What is so important that we would choose to hold onto it as a way of defying an act of love? Do we love God and others enough to make the changes necessary to reach them with the love of God as shown through Christ's church? Is it the order of worship? Is it the way we dress? Is it the way we process in on Sunday morning? What is it we are not willing to let go of in the name of love as we reclaim the gospel message of love?

Reaching the Next Generation While Not Forgetting This Generation

What does it look like to engage in an intentional process of change that is rooted in the gospel? To have a change process rooted in the gospel is one that understands something(s) must die so that we can live and so that others may receive Christ. It is a change process driven by love and not our personal agendas. We love enough to change so that the work of God's church will go on after our time has passed. We love enough to die to self and personal agendas so we can be effective in reaching the next generation for Christ. We move beyond form and fashion and return to the mission of the church as our guide into the future. We face the fact that most of our churches aren't reaching our youth and young adults, and we make it our business to reach them. If we don't reach the next generation for Christ, there will be no one to lead the churches we will leave them. The old churches will die, the property will be sold, and the tradition will be lost. Are we willing to kill what we built, or do we want to be a part of God's revival and resurrection of the church?

Many young adults see the church as nonessential in their lives and faith journey. "Young adults are likely to stay in church if they see church as essential to their lives. . . . But the reality is that most churches in America are doing little to become essential to the lives of their members. Indeed, church is seen by most young adults today as but one option among many for their lives. It is no more important than work, leisure activities, or simply doing nothing."[5] The question that surfaces here is, How do we become relevant in the lives of young adults? Are we willing to develop ministries with them that help them navigate their life journey? Are we willing to employ them in the leadership of the church? Are we willing to make room for them on the boards and committees of the church? What do they need from the church that the church isn't offering?

At the same time that we seek to reach youth and young adults, we are not to forget the needs of our mature adults and seniors. The ministry of reaching populations we aren't reaching is not to be put in competition with meeting the needs of our existing base.

We have to consider capacity as we seek to reach out and reach in. What can we realistically do? In the end we may have to retire some ministries so that we can reallocate resources into birthing new ministries that fit this age and the demographic we aren't reaching. The process of reallocation is a part of the change process, but this isn't a competition of old versus new. It is a call to being faithful to the call of the gospel in this age. The call of the gospel is the appropriate lens by which to have this conversation about resources and ministry development. What does the call of the gospel require of us? How do we show the love of God by what we fund and support? How is our mission reflected in our budget? What does love look like in our ministry profile? Who does our ministry serve? Are we a church with ministries that really help people (of all ages) get closer to God? Can people connect with God and God's liberative mission in the world through our ministries?

What we hear from many young adults is that "I am spiritual but not religious." Interpretation: "I believe in God, but your institution called church isn't getting me closer to God and God's liberative mission in the world. I want to be a part of something that empowers me to have an experience and deep relationship with God, and I want to be a part of a faith community that is about doing real ministry, in the real world, that is making a real difference."

What we know is that 84 percent of African American young adults believe that God exists; 90 percent agree that God's existence does or would affect the way they live; 80 percent believe that God is the God of the Bible.[6] They believe in our God, but they don't believe in our churches. The church has to seek to connect with them, not merely to fill pews or pay bills, but the church must seek to connect them with the God they believe in. This connection means we are going to have to learn to communicate with them in the ways in which they understand and do ministry in this new world we live in. The world has changed, and we have to do ministry in this changed world.

What we know is that young African Americans want to be active in a church that cares, that loves in action, that preaches and teaches in such a way that the Word is relevant and empowering for everyday living. They want to connect in small groups and learn about the Bible in ways that they can understand, digest, and apply to their daily walk:

> Eighty-four percent [of young adult African Americans] agreed they would attend a church that presented truth to them in an understandable way that relates to life now, 69 percent would be willing to join a small group to learn about the Bible and Jesus, 76 percent would be influenced to attend a church that cared about them, and 50 percent would be influenced by the choice of music.[7]

What do we do with this data? Maybe we ask ourselves, Are we doing this? Young adults are not asking us to deny our traditions or not to teach the Word of God. They are not asking us to not be the church. Instead, they are asking to be what we once were. They are asking us to reclaim our roots and be that missional movement that birthed our historic denominations. Young adults are asking us to be what we have been, to be the African American church, the church that empowers, loves, cares, and acts in such a way that we are relevant to the everyday struggles and challenges they face. They want to connect with God and existing church members in real relationships that make a lasting difference in their lives.

Young adults don't want to take over the church from older adults, but rather they want to connect with older adults. They want relationships that matter. They only want us to care, to show them love. We show them love by working with them to develop a church that includes them, makes room for them, and develops ministries with them that connect them with God, the church, and the community in real, meaningful ways.

New Day = New Way

I remember the days of Kodak cameras. I would take my pictures, take the film to a little photo hut, get the film developed, and share my pictures with family and friends. Now I take my pictures with my phone; I don't develop them, but rather I post them on Facebook or Flickr or email them to family and friends. Doug Pagitt would say my new picture-sharing habit is a sign of the times we live in, and he calls this age the "Inventive Age."

> The Inventive Age is one in which inclusion, participation, collaboration, and beauty are essential values. The values of the previous ages still exist, but in different, even subservient, roles. . . . This is the age of Pandora, where I tell an online radio station what to play. It is an age of the App Store, where a major corporation hands control over to an open-source network of ordinary people. It is an age of Wikipedia, where anyone can decide what a world of concept or cultural touchstone means. It

is an age when a bunch of college kids create a social network and six years later it has more 250 million users. It is the age of ownership and customization and user created content.[8]

What does this mean for the church and ministry? It means that one size *doesn't* fit all. Ministry as it has historically been birthed and presented will not work in this age. People don't want things done for them; they want things done with them. They expect to be a part of the process. They will not accept, "We have always done it this way." They expect to participate in discovering new, more effective ways to do ministry. They expect to be part of the process to invent new ways, to do new things that make a real difference. They want to work with you, not for you. They want to serve with you, not under you. They want to ask questions, not be lectured to. They want to engage and think, not be told what to think. They want space for theological inquiry, not Sunday school curriculum. They want to ask what the Bible says, not be told what the Bible said. The expectations have changed. The times have changed. We have to live in this change, and as we live in it, the process will reform us and make us what God would have us to be.

The Inventive Age is an age where people are designed to participate. The vision comes through us, not to us from the pastor. For the church, this will require reorientation and reconfiguration as to how we are organized and how we include people in the process of developing the church's ministry agenda. The Inventive Age is always looking for what is next, new, better, more relevant, and empowering. The target is always moving. The annual programs don't make sense in this age. It is a restless period that thrives on the creative, inventive, collaborative engagement.

The result of this process is a democratization of ministry that demands inclusion of all people, regardless of age, education, gender, and social standing. It is not a bottom-up approach; rather, it is an across-the-board approach. A perfect example of what I am saying takes me back to my time as the pastor to young adults and our Bible studies. We moved from me lecturing for an hour and then opening up the floor for questions to us starting with questions, having a discussion around Scripture, their lives, and popular culture. It was about us studying the Scriptures together, in conversation with their journey, and applying that Word in such away that it made sense for them. And we were doing it together.

This was a complete turnaround from what I had done for years and had been taught to do while in seminary. This experience opened my eyes to what had changed. We have moved to a fully participatory model. This approach of inclusion informed how we planned, led, developed programs, and managed the ministry. This approach of participation and inclusion freed me to do the new stuff. All the weight was no longer on me.

It Is OK to Grieve

When I reflect on my new way to engage Scripture with young adults, I must admit that I lost the way I used to do Bible study. I missed the way I had done it. I enjoyed the old way, and I thought I was pretty good at it. But I had to grieve this loss, to move on and adapt if I wanted to connect.

In this time of change, people not only must be allowed to grieve but also must be encouraged to grieve. Much of what appears to be anger and acting out is grief in disguise. We have to treat it as such and comfort those who are grieving, remembering that it might be you, just as it was me. The way we have known church is changing. This hurts. We have to acknowledge the loss and grieving process. I love to hear the call to worship, process down the aisle, and see the choir in the choir stand with those robes that match my robe. Does this have to change? Maybe, maybe not, but it is on the table.

I don't want to digress into changing the dress code as being the key difference maker. The change we are calling for is much bigger than dress code. I use the dress code because it is obvious, and we can see it. The larger issue is that people want an experience and relationship with God, and they want be a part of a faith community that cares and is making a real difference in their lives and the larger world. To show up on Sunday morning, Wednesday night for Bible study, have a few outreach programs, and say we have done it, will not get it. We have to go back to our mandated biblical mission and assess our faithfulness.

Our barometers of success can no longer be buildings, budgets, and butts in seats. We have to look at the lives that are affected and changed and at the connections they are making inside and outside the walls of the church. The impact a congregation has on the community is as important as the number of people who come down the aisle to give their lives to Christ. We have to employ a new barometer if we are going to be faithful in this age.

What would that new barometer look like? What would it include? It could include

> how many ministry initiatives we are establishing in the streets, how many conversations we are having with pre-Christians, how many volunteers we are releasing into local and global mission projects aimed at community transformation [doing the work of establishing God's justice], how many congregations are starting to reach different populations [or different segments of your present population], how many congregations use our facilities, how many languages (ethnic and generational) we worship in, how many community groups use our facilities, how many church activities target people who aren't here yet, how many hours per week members spend in ministry where they work, go to school, and get mail.[9]

When we change what we count, we change our focus. What are we counting now? What report is the pastor given on Sunday? Is it amount raised, number who attended, number of visitors, and how many joined? That was my old score card or barometer. To be a new church in a new age, we have to look at new marks that will make us that church. What we are counting tells us what counts for our congregation. What are you counting?

Now It's Time to Celebrate

We are living in the best of times. God is going to use us to revive God's church. Future generations are going to look back at this time as a historic moment. It is not a time of great individual leaders, but rather it is going to be us, the masses, doing the work. Our names will not be on marquees; we will not be named in the history books individually, but the roll that will be called will be the people of this age. We are the ones who will answer the call, and God will use us to make the difference.

Fifteen Questions (One More Time)

1. Who are we really as a congregation? Not what our church motto or mission statement says, but who are we really?
2. How would we describe our church?
3. How would a visitor describe our church?
4. How would a young adult child, niece, or nephew describe our church?
5. Do we want to grow? (Remember growth means change; radical growth means radical change.)
6. Do we want be a different church ten years from now? Why or why not?
7. How much change are we willing to initiate and sustain?
8. What are we not willing to change? Why?
9. What is not on the table? Why?
10. When we look at what is not on the table, the question becomes, why *isn't* it on the table? Do we have a biblically principled rationale for not having it on the table?
11. What are our obstacles to growth and change?
12. What are the traditions that served us well in the past that don't serve us well in the present age?
13. What comes first—our Christian identity and Scripture or our denominational identity?
14. Are we Baptists (insert your denomination) who are Christian or are we Christians who are Baptist (insert your denomination)?
15. How am I going be an active supportive participant in the process?

Notes

1. George Barna, *Revolution* (Carol Stream, IL: Tyndale, 2005), 41.
2. Frank Viola and George Barna, *Pagan Christianity?: Exploring the Roots of Our Church Practices* (Carol Stream, IL: Tyndale, 2008), xix.
3. Barna and Viola 13.
4. Gabe Lyons, *The Next Christians: How a New Generation Is Restoring the Faith* (New York: Doubleday, 2010), 192.
5. Thom S. Rainer and Sam S. Rainer III, *Essential Church? Reclaiming a Generation of Dropouts* (Nashville: B&H Publishing Group, 2008), 5.
6. Ed Stetzer, Richie Stanley, and Jason Hayes, *Lost and Found: The Younger Unchurched and the Churches That Reach Them* (Nashville: B&H Publishing Group, 2009), 23.
7. Stetzer, Stanley, and Hayes, 39.
8. Doug Pagitt, *Church in the Inventive Age* (Minneapolis: Sparkhouse Press, 2010), 30.
9. Reggie McNeal, *The Present Future: Six Tough Questions for the Church* (San Francisco: Jossey-Bass, 2003), 67.

6

Alive or Dead?

Locating the Church's Mission in a New World

JUSTIN G. WEST

At the beginning of the book Dr. Watkins and I offered a description of what would make the African American church dead or alive. We noted that one of the methods to gauge the life of the African American church depends on how well it is engaging society as a witness of Christ. This chapter assumes that in order to engage society, the church must become informed about society. Therefore, we want to highlight a few contemporary trends and issues that the church would do well to address in order to be an effective witness to society.

Let me start by acknowledging that the culture of any society is not static but dynamic and often changing rapidly. Society, in fact, is always in a process of becoming. It is taking on new faces every day, every minute, and every second. Even now, as I write, changes are occurring that won't be accounted for in this section. Nonetheless, I invite you into a dialogue about society. If we may, let us frame the discussion by asking a couple of general questions: What changes are facing contemporary society? And what is the trajectory in which society seems to be moving?

I will attempt to provide a brief discussion of some of the significant changes taking place that confront society and that I believe the church must address and develop biblically and socially conscious responses to if the church is to be a pertinent witness of the gospel and a relevant voice in contemporary society. If both the prophetic and praise sides of the African American church are going to reach younger generations specifically, they must grapple with understanding and caring deeply about the issues that involve these generations. It is our aim here to provide resources for the African American church so that it can do all that is within its powers to prevent young men and women from thinking the church to be out-of-touch, irrelevant, or obsolete.

Virtual Life

Letters, phone calls, and physical visits are in a precarious situation, and the reason for this is simple: Social media have replaced them and become the dominant way for millions of people to stay connected and in communication with each other. When we examine the statistics, we see, for instance, that the leading social network, Facebook, has more than 1.15 billion users, a number that is growing every day. In fact, by the time you read this book, the number could top 1.5 billion users. And Facebook isn't alone; other social media networks boast millions of users also. Social media are here, and most reports indicate that they will remain here for a significant part of the foreseeable future.

But what have social media to do with the church? The emergence of social media has not happened without the African American church paying close attention and discerning how it can appropriate this virtual life for ministry. With many church members already participating individually in these social networks, some churches have begun to use some forms of social media for various purposes in their ministries. At my home church, St. John AME Church, my pastor commended our Facebook administrator after a former member, now located in another part of the country, called to thank him for the sermon. According to my pastor, upon inquiring of the member, "Were you at church on Sunday?" the member responded along the lines, "No, but I *was* on Facebook." Indeed, my local congregation is not alone in engaging social media for ministry. But I hesitate to believe that the majority of African American churches use it or know much at all about the various ways to employ it. Some churches may know little to nothing about social media. Others may know about it through research but shy away from using such technology when it comes to the church and ministry. After all, aren't there legitimate concerns about virtual relationships, church, and ministry? Couldn't it lead to replacing face-to-face interactions and ministry?

Bearing in mind each of these situations, let's engage in transparent discussion about the issues involved and raise relevant questions for our churches to consider as they think critically about the world of virtual life and social media, as well as how to minister to people who use it habitually.

Describing Virtual Life

One of the first steps that the African American church can take in order to better understand and therefore be able to relate to generations who have spent significant portions of their life connected to virtual life is to know more about it. Becoming familiar with it and learning how people use it is essential to thinking creatively about ways the church can speak to the issues facing today's society and the younger generations in particular. To help ignite the process for those who don't know where to start, let's begin with a short description of the popular social media networks and how they are used. But first, a quick note: because social media continue to boom each day, it is difficult to account for all of the networks or even those just about to kick off. Therefore, please do not consider this an exhaustive list but only a guide to help start discussion.

Facebook and MySpace: these popular social networks enable people to stay connected to the persons with whom they intend keeping in contact. They provide a range of features that give current and relevant information about what's happening in the lives of family, friends, colleagues, and organizations. They also allow you to send messages (much like email), announcements, and invitations to events, as well as offer updates on your life that you want your networks to know about. In addition, you can share pictures, video, and music within these communities.

Linkedin: created for professional social networking, it permits job seekers to post résumés and explore employment opportunities while allowing employers and businesses to seek potential employees by receiving ready access to profiles. It further gives an option for users to purchase a premium upgrade that places their résumés and profiles first in a long list of others. It is possible for users to follow companies or organizations, or to join groups that reflect their professional skills or interests.

Twitter: a social network that was popularized by its instant message feature that allows users to give brief, informal statements ("tweets") to their "followers." It also allows users to have ongoing or threaded conversations with their followers about a variety of topics. This network is widely used by diverse groups of people; even news journalists use it as a quick way to provide up-to-date information about what is happening throughout the world.

Tumblr: a network that allows you to share information in a blog or journal format among its community. As is the case with Twitter, you can select to follow various personalities who interest you. From a favorite celebrity, to a social organization, to your friends, you can connect to get updates that they post.

YouTube: a network that allows users to upload videos as well as view uploaded videos. From homemade videos to current news, from sports highlights to music videos, from episodes of TV shows to music playlists, from church programs to academic discussions, this network allows you to access thousands of videos of all sorts. If you happen to miss a show, speech, or news program and don't have DVR, no problem. You are likely to find what you missed on YouTube.

Vimeo: similar to YouTube, only more sophisticated and professional, this network allows users to upload videos of their own and to view videos uploaded by others. This network, unlike YouTube, seems geared to meet the interests of aspiring film students and artists, so you are able to find video footage that has usually been professionally produced and edited.

Other technology sites: Instagram and Flickr are networks that enable users to share photos and videos. Pinterest is a network for photo sharing. Skype is a video conferencing interface that has grown in popularity, not only for personal relationships but also for corporate and organizational use, for interviews and meetings.

Merits

There are many merits of these types of social networks. First, they are usually simple and free ways to stay in touch with family, friends, colleagues, business partners, and others. Users can send out private as well as mass messages to their friends. People can use these networks to disseminate new information quickly and to seek out old friends or distant relatives with whom they may have lost touch. Furthermore, social networks allow family and friends who are geographically distant to stay updated—sharing photos and videos of the new house, the new baby, a graduation or anniversary celebration, a comedic or touching moment in life. Missed the first steps or the priceless reaction to a surprise birthday party? Don't worry; the video is posted online to share and preserve for posterity.

In fact, as I originally typed this paragraph, a student from Kenya was accessing Facebook to get the latest word on what was happening with friends in his homeland. Elsewhere, women and men serving overseas in the military use the technology to stay connected with loved ones at home, with an immediacy and intimacy never before imagined. And companies across the nation (and globe) are researching job applicants via their social networks and cutting costs by hosting video interviews and online meetings via Skype. Political candidates are conducting entire campaigns through the grassroots networks of social media, while special-interest groups are generating buzz for their cause via Facebook and Twitter.

The church can take advantage of social media in many ways. By tapping into their collective creativity, churches could employ these outlets to minister in new and unique ways to reach generations who are growing up plugged in to the Web and social media. One of the ways that the church has already begun using social media has been to spread the gospel to a broad audience, especially those persons who would not otherwise come to church. This could be done by a pastor who tweets a daily Bible verse or a deacon who posts inspirational poetry on his or her Facebook wall. A ministry leader may invite pertinent conversations about the life of the church through a thread online, while a church administrator could announce an upcoming wedding or recent birth of a child to keep church members in touch with one another's life events. And of course, churches can regularly update their social media presence with information about church events and fellowship opportunities.

Another way some churches have made the most of social media is by hosting alternative online church services. For instance, some churches stream their worship services live for persons to experience and feel a sense of participation. Other churches have made virtual worship even more complex social spaces that allow persons to give online, to pray with persons online, and to connect with other members through chat rooms or Facebook groups.

In many instances, churches report positive results of the more sophisticated uses of social media. For example, church members who are physically unable to attend worship on Sunday mornings can participate and feel that they are a part of the community and corporate worship. But as congregations continue to utilize and reach people through social media, what will be the long-term significance and legacy of virtual ministry? What are the risks involved? What will its presence mean for face-to-face ministry? Will the benefits outweigh the risks?

Dangers

Despite the wonderful things churches are able to do through various forms of social media, we should also be aware of several dangers. One crucial thing to remember is that whatever gets put on the Web usually has the potential to be viewed by and influence a huge audience. Additional wisdom is provided by Tumblr's "Terms of Service" as of March 3, 2012: "One thing you should consider before posting: When you make something publicly available on the Internet, it becomes practically impossible to take down all copies of it." This means that as the church uses social media to connect to people, it must be careful about how it projects itself and how it presents the gospel. The Web is an accessible outlet for people to view your church, but it is also an easy outlet to make your church look better than it is in reality or to make the gospel look worse than it is. In other words, there is a temptation to portray a false self-image on the Web that disguises what you actually are like or what you actually do; it's what we might call false advertising, such as when an item looks delicious on a menu but arrives at your table appearing nothing like the picture. Or you might put something permanently on the Web that tarnishes your witness and causes lasting regret.

A second issue to consider is if virtual church can have the same effectiveness that the physical church has. In other words, to what extent can an online community be a real community? Are people authentically connected to each other via the Web? Can the virtual church have the same influence on a person's life through its ministries on the Web that it has traditionally had? Admittedly, physical ministry has its miscues and mishaps and mistakes. Sometimes the gospel ministry is not embodied or proclaimed by churches as it should be in the physical sense. But is it always a better alternative than virtual life? Or should tangible ministry and virtual ministry be seen as co-dependents or as complementary in today's age, where not having one or the other limits the scope of effective ministry? How might virtual ministry expand your ministry?

Further Questions to Consider

As your church thinks about these ways to connect through social media, here are some helpful questions to discuss:

1. What is your church saying about virtual life through preaching and Christian education?
2. How is your church using social media (for announcements, church information, marketing, ministry), and why?
3. How authentic is your church on the Web? To what extent does your website reflect who you actually are?
4. How can your church do ministry through social media?
5. Who is managing your church's social media? Are there people holding them accountable?
6. How is information on your sites updated and confirmed for accuracy (if at all)?

Sexuality

Sexuality is not a new topic in society. But depending on any given point in history, there are certain issues regarding sexuality that seem to become more pertinent to a society and begin to define how a society thinks and acts in relation to sexuality. Because sex is glamorized, put constantly on display, and idolized in our contemporary culture, the church cannot ignore this issue. For our discussion of sex and sexuality, it would be helpful for the church to consider a couple of basic questions: What are the major trends and threaded discussions in our contemporary society around sexuality? How do our churches think, talk, and provide instruction concerning larger society's opinions of sex?

But first a simple preliminary question seems appropriate: Is sexuality (encompassing one's gender, sexual organs and the use of them, sexual orientation, and social-emotional-physical interactions with others to whom one is sexually attracted) a proper or fitting topic to discuss within our churches? Let's be honest: for some, if not many, of our churches, sex and sexuality are considered taboo topics. For multiple reasons, we go about our church buildings without creating a space to have any serious engagement or critical discussion of sexuality. We are silent. But is silence healthy to our communities? Is silence contributing to the development of the sexuality that God intends us to have? Some would argue that silence has been harmful to persons within the church. But should the church be a (or perhaps, *the*) place where Christians discuss issues related to homosexuality and bisexuality, transgender, premarital sex, sexual desires, and sexual interactions? Or should these issues be brought up only in other places—home, school, television, and the Internet? Should the church leave it up to society to instruct its congregations on sexuality?

Sexuality is part of our identities as God's creatures, and it is something that God created as well as intends us to be responsible stewards of. While not every sexual desire or action is God-pleasing (and we should discuss what qualifies as such), God nevertheless created us as sexual beings; this means we are supposed to have sexual desires and participate in sexual behavior that pleases the God who created sex. Because sexuality is tied to our identity as God's human beings, part of living as faithful stewards of God's creation implies that we strive to live as responsible sexual thinkers and doers. In other words, we are to be stewards over our physical bodies and sexual identities. But how should the church teach its people to think about sexuality in a culture in which it is pervasive? What instruction should the church provide about sexuality that pleases God?

Creating Spaces for Conversation

Part of the difficulty churches may experience when it comes to discussing sexuality is the problem of when and where to discuss it. Should preachers draw implications for a God-pleasing sexuality from the pulpit? Should Bible studies or small groups talk about this issue? Should churches hand out guides or pamphlets that provide information regarding God and sexuality?

The answer to these questions may be different for local churches. Some may utilize one of these methods, some may utilize all of them, and some may think of alternative ways to get the issue on the discussion table. No matter what method a church takes to initiate the discussion, it seems the most important thing is that the issue becomes discussed in positive, healthy, and constructive ways, perhaps starting with the words "God views sex as good, and we should too."

As the people of God, the church should play a critical role in helping brothers and sisters in Christ understand God's intentions for sexuality. Although sex has not been historically discussed in African American churches, younger generations have become increasingly frustrated about churches not having safe spaces to have honest conversation about this issue while simultaneously being bombarded by society's influences. Having served as a youth minister, I know that youth would often wonder if and when we'd discuss sex and if we'd transparently discuss it. Therefore, it seems that a first step the church must take is creating spaces for Christian discussion and instruction on sexuality to occur on a regular basis.

Framing the Conversation Constructively

In addition to the question of when and where to discuss sexuality is the question of how churches should talk about such an "untouchable" topic. Perhaps at least a few things can be said in this regard.

First, as churches create spaces to discuss issues regarding sexuality, there is a teaching tendency among some churches that seems problematic. That tendency is structuring conversation in such a way that sex gets talked about using either simplistic language or negative terminology. Talking simplistically about sex usually occurs when people harbor the mindset that there are only black and white, yes or no, all or nothing answers to the questions or issues posed in conversation. For example, some people will assume that Scripture offers basic, easily identified principles or responses to contemporary questions about sex and sexuality. For others, though, the Bible is more complex, and when social and historical contexts are taken into account, locating what the Bible has to say for today regarding marriage, sexual interactions outside of marriage, same-sex attractions, and more is extremely challenging.

In a similar way, speaking negatively about sexuality often means a person takes a position that assumes sexuality and sexual activity are mostly immoral; this is usually a result of simplistic thinking and frequently gets framed in terms such as "this is what we shouldn't do," "this is immoral behavior," "you should avoid this," or "just say no!"

I am not suggesting that there is not a place for black-and-white answers or for speaking negatively about sex (for example, some forms of sexual behavior seem more clearly prohibited in Scripture than others), but I am suggesting that the church often misses a few important points. First, simplistic thought and negative speech typically fail to emphasize that sexual expression can include wonderful ways to worship God in our bodies. Second, the church often fails to evaluate the complexity of sexuality and how it affects individuals struggling deeply with certain issues. Thus, what often happens is that in trying to provide quick and concrete answers to certain issues or questions, the church will not recognize that loving a person who is wrestling with sexuality may be better displayed by trying to empathize with a person rather than offering easy, simplistic, or negative answers. Consequently, quick and dogmatic answers may lead to more harmful or devastating situations and risky sexual behavior for individuals who become repelled by the church.

Returning to the analogy above, if our bodies and sexuality (psychoemotional and physical) are gifts from God, how can the church responsibly teach appropriate sexual stewardship? How do we disciple young people about their development and relationships as they mature? How do we empower adults who have stumbled in the area of sexuality to embrace forgiveness, reconciliation, redemption, and repentance? How do we equip parents, mentors, teachers, and leaders to advise, counsel, and nurture healthy sexuality and responsible choices in self and others?

With this in mind, my suggestion is that the church learn to frame conversations regarding sexuality in constructive ways (see discussion starters below), starting with a positive discussion of sex, moving into transparent dialogue that encourages patient listening, and abstaining from quick and simplistic answers.

Questions to Consider

The issues regarding sex and sexuality are myriad. Below are some questions that may be discussion starters. With each question, we should consider why we answer it a certain way (for example, were we taught this?) and what Scripture references might inform our responses. We should also seek to frame the conversation positively. In other words, we should do so in a loving and edifying way that doesn't seek to cast judgment or condemn anyone. We are shooting for an honest and open conversation about how God views, and how we should view, sex and sexuality.

1. What type of sex pleases God?
2. What is marriage in this day and age?
3. How should we think about premarital sex?
4. Is cohabitating with a committed partner okay? What about prior to marriage? Why or why not?
5. What about singleness and sexuality? Can single people have sex, including those who are single again (divorced or widowed)?
6. What qualifies as lust? What qualifies as sexual immorality?
7. What are GLBT (gay-lesbian-bisexual-transgender) issues? How should we view and relate to people who identify themselves in one of these categories?
8. How should we restore people hurt sexually in any type of way?

Race Matters in a Postracial Age?

In a conversation with one of my mentors, a pastor of an AME church, we began to discuss the issue of how people think about race in today's society. After talking specifically about how younger generations are beginning to view race, he went on to make a statement that was quite revealing of some of the current perceptions of the meaning of race. He related a comment made by one of his mentors, an eighty year-old African American male and elder in our church, to him. "Soon everybody's going to be colored," his mentor remarked.

What did he mean by this? To put it simply, this African American elder meant that society has become so racially integrated and populated with racially mixed persons that sooner than later the racial categories that we use to define each other's skin color (black, white, yellow, red) might become obsolete. The words *black* and *white* might start to mean less and less or become meaningless. Evidence of this trajectory can be found in the latest report conducted by the U.S. Census Bureau, which states that from 2000 to 2010 interethnic married couples increased by more than 28 percent, with many additional interethnic couples cohabitating.[1] Although the elder's statement may not be completely reflective of where society is moving regarding "race thinking," it nevertheless serves as a good example of the complexity of race in our day and age.

In this short section we want to raise two questions for us to consider together regarding the complexity of race in the twenty-first century. First, it is important to ask what trajectory society is moving regarding how it thinks about and operates regarding one's race. Second, we must ask what this means for the identity of the African American church, and especially the way in which it relates to African American people.

Race Trajectories

Although the socially invented term "race" has always been a problematic way to categorize and characterize a group of people, it is facing new complexities as it is used to describe people in North America today. This is no less true than it is for people with "black" or dark skin (or African ancestry). In this section we offer a few key terms to open up the discussion of where black people find themselves in current times. Is society today racist, postracial, or somewhere in the middle?

For the last decade or more, there has been hot debate among the general public as well as among African Americans regarding the existence of racism. We are particularly concerned with the debate within the African American community. One the one side are those who hold that racism still exists, although more covertly than before, usually occurring on an institutional or systemic level. In other words, while people won't generally discriminate against persons with certain skin colors on an individual basis, institutions and systems frequently do, which is reflected in job opportunities, quality of education, housing, criminal justice, and more. For this group, to varying degrees African Americans and other people of color continue to be treated unjustly and suffer exclusion from certain sectors of society.

Other African Americans position themselves on the other side of the debate, viewing racism as virtually nonexistent (though some might still admit that there are pockets of racism in America). These folks are usually but not exclusively those who have achieved financial success or members of the younger generations who have developed in multicultural and middle- to upper-class environments. This group of African Americans typically suggests that we live in an increasingly postracial society in which one is no longer treated a certain way based on one's skin color. From their viewpoint, African Americans have equal opportunities to progress in society that anyone else may have, including access to the best education, jobs, resources, and housing available; they might point to blacks who have significant accomplishments in business or politics, especially those who hold positions of great influence or power in society—often citing President Barack Obama as the prime example.

But which side of the debate is "right"?

Progress, Racism, or Class Divisions?

When we argue one way or the other regarding whether race matters or if racism still persists, one's opinion is usually tainted by one's personal experience. That inherent subjectivity reveals another important point to discussing race, namely, that while both sides of the debate usually make arguments that contain at least some truth, the whole truth is inevitably more complex and multifaceted than the experience of a single individual, family, or neighborhood. And one element typically missing from contemporary debates around race is a discussion of classism and how one's socioeconomic class influences one's view of racial dynamics.

As cultural critic bell hooks contends powerfully in *Where We Stand*,[2] we live in a society in which classism is prevalent and may become a more powerful force than racism. Her argument sheds light on why wealthy blacks, who have spent much time in affluent, multicultural settings where they had the same opportunities as whites, might suggest that racism exists minimally, while working-class blacks still living in a homogenous black community with scarce resources might think racial discrimination persists. To put it another way, hooks recognizes a diversity among African Americans that is not often addressed but often is played out in a discussion of race. Thus, African Americans who have made it financially and professionally may have a tendency to look down upon those who remain impoverished or financially vulnerable by suggesting that working-class blacks should work harder and quit using racism as an excuse for their lack of "success."

Diversity among African Americans and Black Churches

So, where does the African American church find itself in a present-day discussion of race? How should the African American church think of its relationship to "the African American community" when that community is increasingly diverse in geography and socioeconomic status? With a growing middle and upper class of African Americans, whose experience far exceeds the misery and oppression of past generations and their working-class brothers and sisters, is the church still the refuge, social center, and gathering grounds for African Americans? Or has it become something else?

Certainly the church must think carefully about these issues and respond to them in a loving manner. It must realize that racial rhetoric even among African Americans is so complex that all sides need to be heard and felt sincerely before any stance is taken. For example, the church must honor the reasons that some African Americans praised Viola Davis and Octavia Spencer for their remarkable performances in the 2011 movie *The Help*, just as it acknowledges those who criticized the actresses for playing roles that were considered complicit in perpetuating degrading stereotypes and opening old wounds. Perhaps more than anything, the church must bear in mind that to be an African American in today's culture means, more than ever before, different things for different groups of African Americans, and the same might be true for the African American church.

More Questions for Discussion

1. Does race still matter in society? Why or why not?
2. Does race still matter in our specific community? Why or why not?
3. How would our church function in a postracial society, if such exists?
4. How should our church think about race?
5. How is our church adapting to minister in an increasingly cosmopolitan society in which mixed-race persons are becoming a more common presence (or at least an acknowledged presence) in society?
6. How can our church preserve its history while still being relevant to generations who think differently about race?
7. What features make a church authentically African American? To what extent (if at all) is "African American" a necessary nomenclature for a majority black church? Why?

Shifting Communities

In the history of African American churches, we learned that their establishment occurred within and on behalf of black communities across the United States. As church historians have repeatedly pointed out, our churches have not functioned in the communities only as religious or spiritual bodies, but they have served a variety of functions. For this reason, church historians have previously called the African American church the social service center or community center within the black community.[3]

But over time, significant changes have redefined what once defined the African American community in some cities—so much so that when I asked a pastor of a large church outside of Atlanta about how his church is addressing issues of the black community, he responded, "Where is the black community? It doesn't exist."

Although many African American churches have remained physically situated within primarily black communities, over the past several decades, urban demographics have been shifting in such ways that many churches are beginning to see historically black communities experience transformations of a variety of shapes. One of these transformations has been the departure of the black middle and upper classes.

Partly as a result of African Americans integrating further into society and gaining access to more privileges (such as moving to historically "white only" neighborhoods), many black professionals have moved out of black communities in the heart of the city to the suburbs—a move that characterized wealthy whites nearly decades before them. While social scientists have noticed the detrimental effect this shift has had on the quality of education and economic stability of black communities, a question that has been largely overlooked is how the loss also affects the existence and role of the African American churches that remain.

A more recent phenomenon that has been affecting the churches has been a process called gentrification. This term is used to describe a situation whereby city policies allow for the renewal of certain city properties. Because the renewal results in an increase in rent and property value, many established residents are unable to afford continued occupancy of their residences. The consequence of this inability to meet the costs of living in gentrified areas is that many poor black residents are forced to leave their communities and find occupancy in other parts of the city. Naturally, the dislocation of blacks from historically black communities and the arrival of other ethnic groups have altered the demographics of the communities where many black church buildings still remain.

With the departure of black professionals as well as those forced out by gentrification, African American churches that remain face several important questions regarding their ministry. Perhaps the most pressing question is what will be the church's identity and purpose within the shifting demographics of their communities. In some cities, although church members have moved away from the neighborhood, these members return to the neighborhood for church gatherings. In these situations, churches have become predominately commuter congregations and the church membership no longer reflects the demographics of the current community. A potential result of this reality is that the churches may become disengaged and unconcerned about these communities.

While some churches have responded to demographic changes by becoming commuter churches, the result for other churches has been empty church buildings. In other words, relocation and dislocation of blacks from where they had historically resided in the city has, at least to some degree, led to a decline of attendance and participation in some churches. And there seem to be at least two reasons for this numerical decline in church attendance. First, blacks who have moved away have either chosen not to return to the city for church (perhaps because of the people who are in the community) or cannot return for any number of reasons. Second, persons who have remained in the community, and the new residents of other cultural and ethnic backgrounds who have become a part of the community, are also not attending.

So what is the church to do? What is the church's task in the midst of these shifting demographics? How will African American churches in historically black communities relate to the people who now live in their communities, as well as to the people who have moved or been forced away? Would it be appropriate for these churches to make significant changes to their identity in order to attract people of many different backgrounds to their church? Should churches uproot and resituate themselves in black communities outside of the city? These are among the crucial questions that churches in contemporary society face regarding shifting demographics of the city. And there are yet more questions to consider:

1. Who makes up our current community?
2. What is the church's role in its specific community?
3. What is God's mission for our church as it pertains to our current neighbors?
4. What does it mean to be a commuter church, and what are the challenges that face commuter churches?
5. Should the church move to a new location if the majority of its members have left the community? Why or why not?

Notes

1. www.census.gov (accessed September 9, 2013).
2. bell hooks, *Where We Stand: Class Matters* (New York: Routledge, 2000).
3. See chapter 3.

7

Death or Resurrection

Social Issues, Moral Crisis

RALPH BASUI WATKINS

There is a call on the church of this age to reassess what social issues it must engage. It is not the church of the civil rights generation, but it is a child of the civil rights generation. The church of the civil rights age was clear about the issues it addressed, which were primarily the issues of Jim Crow. The questions before us are, What is the new Jim Crow? What are those issues that we must pay attention to, be informed about, and deal with head-on?

In this chapter we introduce some of the major social problems, with resources for further study, as we invite churches to seek God in how God is calling their church to respond to issues such as the prison industrial complex, public education, healthcare, the growing underclass, hyper-ghettoized communities, single-parent homes, teen pregnancy, gangs, violence, suicide, drug addiction, and divorce. This is not an exhaustive list, and yours might be different from ours. The point here is not to prioritize as much as it is an attempt to try to identify the new Jim Crow(s), which might not be as obvious as signs on segregated water fountains and lunch counters. It is our hope that congregations will discuss these issues as they relate to their context and then move to action. The community is looking to the church for leadership, and we believe that you are going to lead!

Let me be clear: this chapter is not intended as a polemic against praise churches or a letter only to exhort prophetic churches. The African American church of today needs to embrace both ends of this continuum from praise to prophetic. Sunday mornings need to be liberative experiences of praise because we need the release that worship offers, but we can't stop there. We have to be empowered in worship to serve as liberative agents in the world on Monday through Saturday. The separation between worship and social activism must be eliminated from our thinking. The two are connected. Social activism that leads to real-world liberation from real problems is what gives us a reason to worship. The work of the church is to dismantle systemic structures of injustice. Being a part of God's prophetic and liberative work in the world gives us reason to praise.

The Interconnectedness of Social Problems

To identify the top ten social problems is tricky. It gets us into thinking that these are the only issues, so we put them on our agenda and begin to attack them one by one. Let's not fall for the illusion that it is possible to fix an issue neatly and discretely before moving on to the next. What we know is that social problems are woven into the very tapestry of our society. We have to see them as interconnected, and the approach to them has to address this interconnectedness.

When we think about the family, as an example, many of my colleagues think the answer is getting the "man back in the home." So we develop a men's ministry to achieve this goal. There is nothing wrong with having a men's ministry, but it isn't the answer by itself. If men are absent from the homes we think they should share with their children and significant other, then we have to ask what are the myriad issues affecting the stability of homes where both parents live together and are active in the lives of their children. The answer to this question is more complex than developing a men's ministry.

When we look beyond the simplistic, prescriptive approach to addressing social problems, we will see how complex they are and therefore how multifaceted our approach to dealing with them has to be. The issue of absentee fathers is not resolved by getting men to a Saturday morning meeting or prayer breakfast. It isn't even fixed merely by restoring those men to a relationship with God. This issue is linked to the school system, which is linked to the employment system, which is linked to the justice system, which is linked to the many negative messages African American men get from popular culture, which is linked to the breakdown of the basic building blocks of strong communities.

If I am right about these interrelated issues, we see the men's ministry as one of many things we need to identify and address if we hope to have parents living together in monogamous relationships, sharing the duties of raising strong children and developing strong families.

This insight is not meant to overwhelm us or even to suggest that the local church alone has to solve all of the interconnected problems. What I am hoping is that we see the complexity of the problems and not think in reductionist solutions. The problems are deeper and more complex than they appear, and therefore, they demand that churches look at these relationships and devise a strategy to address them that are also multifaceted.

From Then to Now: Looking Back as We Turn to Look Forward

What we are talking about in this chapter isn't new. Dr. Martin Luther King Jr. was calling us to this ministry at the end of his life. When Dr. King was murdered in Memphis, Tennessee, on April 4, 1968, he was on his way to Washington to begin leading the Poor People's Campaign. The road to Washington took a turn through Memphis in support of the black sanitation workers' strike, which was born on February 11, 1968, ironically on the eve of Abraham Lincoln's birthday.

> The call from Memphis caught King and the SCLC in full-swing preparation for the Poor People's Campaign. Hesitant to add to the SCLC's agenda at a time when support for its own April campaign was flagging, King was reluctant at first but finally relented. The civil rights leader could not flinch in the face of human needs, and after all, the plight of Black sanitation workers was in microcosm the Poor People's Campaign itself.[1]

King was calling for an end to the war in Vietnam and a redirection of those resources to dismantle an unjust socioeconomic structure in the United States. After the death of King, his followers would attempt to continue the call by mounting a movement in Washington, D.C., represented by the establishment of Resurrection City on May 12, 1968. (Resurrection City was a shantytown with its own zip code and as many as three thousand occupants, which stood on the National Mall for six weeks, until cleared by city officials.) The Economic Bill of Rights that King was championing prior to his death was never passed. In essence the movement was stopped in its tracks.

In Michael Eric Dyson's *April 4, 1968: Martin Luther King Jr.'s Death and How It Changed America*, he makes a convincing argument that after the death of King, the soul of the movement was lost. The soul of the movement lay in a grave in South View Cemetery in Atlanta, Georgia, and his successors failed to lead the war on poverty. Since then, the church has sought the successor to King. The irony of the quest is that none of King's contemporaries were able to fill that role.

In Dyson's chapter 4, "Report Card on Black America," the social analyst makes it clear: Black America is worse off forty-some years after the death of Dr. King than they were when he was living because the movement has essentially been buried. We aren't here to blame the church for all that hasn't happened. We would simply ask, Are we still looking at the funeral procession of April 9, 1968, waiting for someone to be resurrected? The question on the table is, What are we doing today? We have to move beyond the blame and begin to deal with the what and how of now. How do we move forward in a progressive liberative way in the spirit of Jesus?

A King-Sized Challenge

At the end of Dr. King's life,

> King took the black church to task for being possessed of a religion that talked more than it acted. He criticized religion for adding to, rather than challenging, social suffering. . . . King said from his pulpit a week before his last birthday, "But the problem is that the church has sanctioned every evil in the world. Whether it's racism, or whether it's the evils of monopoly-capitalism, or whether it's the evils of militarism. And this is why these continue to exist in the world today."[2]

I wonder, if Dr. King were here today, what he would say? Are we still possessed with a religion that talks more than it acts? Are we in a religion that even talks about social problems from a systemic perspective? When they had mass meetings during the civil rights movement, those meetings were held in the church. How many mass meetings are being held in churches today? I know there are a lot of conferences, conventions, revivals, workshops, and the like, but what about mass meetings that are focused on changing an unjust stratified society?

In my experience (yours maybe different), in the churches I have served, we have ministered to the poor, but rarely have we challenged the systems that create and maintain poverty. We have given out stuff and we have responded when major turmoil happened in our city, but have we led a movement? No.

> King believed that charity was a poor substitute for justice. Charity is a hit-or-miss proposition; folk who tire of giving stop doing so when they think they've done enough. Justice seeks to take the distracting and fleeting emotions out of giving. Justice does not depend on feeling to do the right thing. It depends on action and sound thinking about the most helpful route to the best and most virtuous outcome. . . . While others made war on poverty, King made war on what made them poor.[3]

This distinction—between making war on poverty as compared with a war on what makes the poor—is significant. For too long we have blamed the poor for their poverty without looking at the larger systemic structures embedded in a stratified society that keeps people poor and subsequently preys on them.

Dismantling the Structures That Keep Us Down

In a stratified society, in order to maintain the socioeconomic order of those at the top and those at the bottom, social structures are put in place to secure the layers as they exist. Those groups who are at the top and those groups who are at the bottom are maintained, generation after generation. How long have the masses of our people been poor? Please don't refer to the small minority of us who have gained some of the signs of wealth; remember, these are the exceptions that prove the rule. Yes, that is what I meant to say: these are the exceptions that prove the rule.

The rule is that masses of our people are stuck on the bottom of America's socioeconomic ladder. Let's be clear what we mean when we use the word *stratification*. Stratification is the social process through which rewards and resources such as wealth, power, and prestige are distributed systematically and unequally within or among societies. It is also based on identifiable social processes through which people are sorted into categories such as socioeconomic class. Stratification differs from simple inequality in that it is systematic.

Sheryl Cashin explains clearly the foundation of the present-day stratified society in *The Failures of Integration: How Race and Class Are Undermining the American Dream* when she says,

> Policy choices gave impetus not just to racially and economically exclusive suburbs but also to the black ghetto. Concentrated black poverty—the form of segregation that has had perhaps the most enduring impact in creating inequality—was by and large a government creation. Under urban renewal programs, begun in 1949 . . . Blacks evicted for the purpose of renewing our nation's downtown centers were forced to move either into existing ghetto neighborhoods or into racially segregated public housing.[4]

There is a root to the causes of what we see in the streets. The class divide is real, systemic, and structural, and it has been maintained for hundreds of years here in the United States. Until we come to grips with the systemic nature of what we see happening in our nation, we will merely serve the poor but never transform systems that create and maintain stratification.

The result of a stratified society is a class system that operates more like a caste system. In a true caste system, there are rigid categories into which people are born with no possibility of change. In an operative caste system, one person may defy all odds and make it out and up, and we are quick to say, "See, you can do it too." However, the reality is that the one person who escapes his or her class-caste proves the rule of the systems as millions of others never make it out or up.

As bell hooks says,

Class matters. Race and gender can be used as screens to deflect attention away from the harsh realities class politics exposes. Clearly when we should be paying attention to class, using race and gender to understand and explain its new dimensions, society, even our government, says let's talk about race and racial injustices. It is impossible to talk meaningfully about ending racism without talking about class.[5]

What happens in the African American community is that we are quick to talk about what it means to be African American and how systemic racism operates—and we need to have that discussion. But we can't have that discussion without factoring in how class works as an operative caste system, which exacerbates the oppression of poor African Americans. We are not trying to factor out racism (and sexism and other -isms) as systemic factors of oppression, but we want to also make sure we don't miss the caste effects of classism.

Responding by Leading:
A Feminist Approach to Liberation

The next logical question is, What should be the foundation of our fight against the injustice our people are presently facing? Let me offer a feminist approach as a starting point for our discussion. Why a feminist approach? The reason is that

> revolutionary feminist thinking has always raised the issue of classism among women. From the onset, there has been a struggle within feminist movement between the reformist model of liberation, which basically demands equal rights for women within the existing class struggle, and more radical and/or revolutionary models, which call for fundamental change in the existing structure so that models of mutuality and equality can replace old paradigms.[6]

The first step for revolutionary feminist struggles is changing the structures in society so that stratification no longer exists. When we seek equality merely in the present structure, equality will never be achieved because the foundation upon which the society is built is already tilted to favor and privilege those it has favored since the founding of this nation. If we birth our movement of the twenty-first century on revolutionary feminist principles, we start with the understanding that the system must be dismantled and rebuilt if equality is to be the dream.

Don't let feminism scare you. Being an African American male preacher, who hangs around a lot of brothers like me, I recognize that sexism has strong roots in our tradition. We have to commit ourselves to become liberated from our sexist ways and embrace a feminist ethic. If we look deeper at what feminism really is we find that

> [a] basic definition of feminism is that it is a movement to end sexism and sexist exploitation and oppression. . . . The only genuine hope of feminist liberation lies with a vision of social change that takes into consideration the ways interlocking systems of classism, racism, and sexism work to keep women exploited and oppressed. . . . In this country the combined forces of a booming prison industry and workfare-oriented welfare in conjunction with conservative immigration politics create the conditions for indentured slavery to be condoned.[7]

One of the keys to this definition is that when we take a feminist position, we begin to see the connections between classism, racism, and sexism. For too long we have focused our movements on dealing head-on with racism, and to some extent, that was understandable. As we move forward, however, we have to begin a conversation that deals frankly with the reality that when you are an African American who is also poor and female, you are fighting against classism, racism, and sexism. These three cords of oppression are bound together. To focus on only one of the interlocking cords misses the link and the ways in which African Americans experience oppression in the United States in the twenty-first century.

The Social Problems We Must Address

During the civil rights era, racism was blatant and we had a common enemy. We could literally see it in the form of water fountains and signs that pointed to the colored section. African American congregations rallied around ending the clear racial divide. While there was disagreement about how fast we should move in addressing these issues (some said "end Jim Crow now" and others argued for gradualism), people generally agreed that Jim Crow was a social problem that had to be addressed.

Today identifying the problem isn't as straightforward, not with the class divide in African American communities being more pronounced by the new geographic divide that didn't exist in the 1950s and 1960s. Back then, housing policies ensured that our cities were racially divided; you could be middle or upper class and you were still subject to living in the "black" community. Today socioeconomic success offers social and physical mobility, which means African Americans are divided by social class, by geography, and by technology (what sociologists have called the digital divide). As a result we see the world very differently, and we see social problems very differently.

I am a black feminist-womanist liberation theologian through and through. Therefore, my theological bent is one that understands the gospel as inherently liberative. Jesus did not come to save our souls and leave our bodies in a living hell. Jesus was clear in Luke 4:18 that he came to set the captives free. When Jesus talked about heaven in Matthew 25:31-46, Jesus was clear that what we have done in the way of achieving social justice is the key question he will ask us on Judgment Day. The church can't live in a world beside oppressive forces and do nothing. If the church does nothing, it is complicit with the oppressive forces by its silence and inaction.

As I was working on this book, I interviewed Rev. Dr. Leslie Callahan, pastor of St. Paul's Baptist Church in Philadelphia, Pennsylvania, and I asked her why is it that African American congregations aren't more vocal on social issues, as we seemed to be during those moments like the civil rights movement. Her analysis was helpful and pushed me to make sure this chapter was in this book.

Dr. Callahan inferred that we haven't taught it. In seminary we don't have that class or core of classes that outlines the derivative of social problems or the development of social movements that challenge and transform unjust social systems in response to those problems. Moreover, she hinted at the fact that we don't have that common enemy anymore, in racism, at least not in the form in which it historically existed so that we could attack it as the obvious enemy. Although racism, sexism, and classism are alive and well, we don't see them as clearly as signs posted on water fountains.

The remainder of this chapter is my ten-point response to Dr. Callahan's answer. These are the ten issues I would introduce in a course on the topic, and some of the resources I would suggest that we study. It is my hope that as you read this section, you will commit to becoming more informed and engaged around the issues by, at a minimum, reviewing the recommended resources as a way to continue the conversation.

1. The Promise of Public Education: The Key to the Door

I would not be a professor if I had not been the beneficiary of a quality public education. Today the promise of public education that prepared me to compete in this world is in jeopardy in cities across the nation. When the budget gets tight, the first thing governments seem to cut are programs that benefit our children, from schools to libraries to public recreation.

Most of our kids have no choice but public education. We cannot be expected to pay taxes, tithes, *and* tuition. Schools of choice and vouchers aren't the answer. If I don't have a car, I can't get my kids to the schools of choice that don't provide bus transportation. After the voucher, how do I pay the additional $10,000 out of my $40,000 salary? School vouchers are no more than a supplement for upper-middle-class families and their children.

This is a class issue. As a poor kid I went to good public schools and got a good education so I could compete with my middle-class classmates in college. The same thing that saved me will save our kids today, and that is a quality public school education. We have to make sure that our public schools are fully funded and supported by our tax dollars. Kids can't learn in underfunded, understaffed, overcrowded schools.

The United States has reverted to what Jonathan Kozol has called the restoration of an "apartheid school system." At the core of Kozol's argument is that our schools are separated along race and class lines, and if you don't believe it, go and see. Visit the schools in your community, and then go across town and visit the other schools. See the inequity for yourself, and report on what you see to your congregation. Pastors and church leaders need to visit the schools and see.

Let me also offer two resources as lens that might assist you to fully understand what and why you see what you see:

- *Another Kind of Public Education: Race, Schools, the Media, and Democratic Possibilities* by Patricia Hill-Collins (Boston: Beacon Press, 2009).
- *The Trouble with Black Boys: . . . And Other Reflections on Race, Equity, and the Future of Public Education* by Pedro A. Noguera (San Francisco: Jossey-Bass, 2008).

2. The New Jim Crow: Unlocking the Chains of Mass Incarceration

Declining quality in public education and the swelling prison industrial complex are problems that are interrelated and connected. Student achievement or lack thereof has a direct correlation as to who winds up in prison. The classroom-to-prison pipeline is real. If kids are empowered in first through twelfth grades, college-ready, they will not find themselves in courtrooms. What is happening in the courtroom is linked to what is not happening in the classroom. And we will say later a big part of this is also what is happening in the home. How do we walk along beside families so that our kids will enter kindergarten ready to learn?

What author and attorney Michelle Alexander has done in *The New Jim Crow: Mass Incarceration in the Age of Colorblindness* is to sound the alarm with the data to back up her cry. We do have a new Jim Crow, but we can't isolate it. We have to see how this new Jim Crow is yet another part of the systemic web of oppression in which our people are caught. In the book, Alexander argues that because the dominant culture now veils racism behind the cloak of the "criminal injustice system," we don't see it as clearly. The rhetoric of being "tough on crime" and "the war on drugs" has resulted in many African Americans not being able to see through the veil. Mass incarceration has replaced Jim Crow and is systematically disenfranchising an entire generation of citizens. Alexander says:

What has changed since the collapse of Jim Crow has less to do with the basic structure of our society than with the language we use to justify it. In the era of colorblindness, it is no longer socially permissible to use race, explicitly, as a justification for discrimination, exclusion, and social contempt. So we don't. Rather than rely on race, we use our criminal justice system to label people of color "criminals" and then engage in all the practices we supposedly left behind. Today it is perfectly legal to discriminate against criminals in nearly all the ways it was legal to discriminate against African Americans. Once you're labeled a felon, the old forms of discrimination—employment discrimination, housing discrimination, denial of the right to vote, denial of educational opportunity, denial of food stamps and other public benefits, and exclusion from jury service—are suddenly legal. As a criminal, you have scarcely more rights, and arguably less respect, than a black man living in Alabama at the height of Jim Crow. We have not ended racial caste in America; we have merely redesigned it.[8]

The United States has essentially redeveloped slavery in our midst. The injustice system is active every day in the same way slave catchers were active on the continent of Africa. Behind the walls of police stations and the closed doors of courtrooms, African Americans are sent to stationary slave ships called prisons and jails every day. The system is inherently racist and classist. The data exposes the inherent discrimination built into the injustice system. Alexander explains,

> What we know is that people of all colors use and sell illegal drugs at similar rates. If there are significant differences to be found, they frequently suggest that whites, particularly white youth, are more likely to engage in drug crime than people of color . . . [but] black men have been admitted to prison on drug charges at rates twenty to fifty times greater that those of white men. . . . In major cities . . . as many as 80 percent of young African American men now have criminal records and are thus subject to legalized discrimination for the rest of their lives. These young men are part of a growing undercaste, permanently locked up and locked out of mainstream society. A caste system

has been developed and the bias in the enforcement of drug laws is one of many examples. This issue of the new slavery in the form of the injustice system has to be on the top of our agenda.[9]

- *The New Jim Crow: Mass Incarceration in the Age of Colorblindness* by Michelle Alexander (New York: The New Press, 2010).
- *Imprisoning America: The Social Effects of Mass Incarceration*, edited by Mary Pattillo, David Weiman, and Bruce Western (New York: Russell Sage Foundation, 2004).
- *Ministry with Prisoners and Families: The Way Forward*, edited by W. Wilson Goode, Charles E. Lewis, and Harold Dean Trulear (Valley Forge, PA: Judson Press, 2012).

3. The Employment Factor: Class Matters

There was a time when you could get your high school diploma, go downtown, and get a career-track, family-sustaining job in manufacturing and textiles the next day, but those days are long gone. We now live in a high-tech service economy that calls for highly educated workers. Not only has the type of employment changed, but also the location has changed. The jobs have moved to the suburbs, and for many working-class African Americans, those jobs are literally out of reach. Scholars such as William J. Wilson argue further that of the jobs that *are* geographically accessible, there aren't enough positions in the city to employ fully the African Americans who live there.

The result of this changing employment arrangement is a permanent underclass or undercaste. This employment reality is most obviously linked to access to quality public education, including public colleges. If this problem is not addressed, we will have a generation of undereducated African Americans who have experienced and will experience long droughts of unemployment, which makes them targets of the injustice system. If we don't act, they will all too soon be enslaved in the prison system.

- *Where We Stand: Class Matters* by bell hooks (New York: Routledge, 2000).

- *When Work Disappears: The World of the New Urban Poor* by William J. Wilson (New York: Vintage, 1997).

4. Home Ownership versus Renting: The New Company Store

When the mortgage crisis hit, African Americans were already far behind their white counterparts when it came to home ownership. It looked like we were making ground, and then the bottom fell out. "The subprime mortgage crisis will cost black folk between $71 billion and $122 billion, the greatest loss of black wealth in history."[10] We lost what we thought we had, and it will take a generation to regain the wealth we lost.

While many congregations tried to help families save their homes (and that was the right thing to do), we can't stop there. We have to look at a banking system and credit system that has robbed African Americans of their wealth potential because of unjust lending practices. At the core of this problem is the dismantling of the black community from a land and home perspective. There can be no African American church without a physical African American community, which requires strong homes and strong families that are supported by a strong education and employment sector.

- *Black Picket Fences: Privilege and Peril Among the Black Middle Class* by Mary Pattillo-McCoy (Chicago: University of Chicago Press, 2013).
- *Blue-Chip Black: Race, Class, and Status in the New Black Middle Class* by Karyn R. Lacy (Berkeley: University of California Press, 2007).

5. Black Business in the Red: Supporting and Developing Black Businesses

We can't have strong African American communities without a viable employment and business sector. Individual African Americans and our churches have to make a conscious effort to develop and support African American businesses. This means we have to counteract the myths and stereotypes about African American–owned businesses, and we have to support them so that they can be what we see in other large chains that we support on a daily basis.

One of the books I recommend for every church to read together is Maggie Anderson's *Our Black Year: One Family's Quest to Buy Black in America's Racially Divided Economy*.[11] I highlight this book because it is a true story of real family who spent their money intentionally and made a difference. One family, one dollar at a time can make a difference. We don't need a movement; we just need to be more intentional about how we spend our nearly one trillion dollars of buying power. The fact is that "less than two cents of every dollar an African American spends in this country goes to Black-owned businesses."[12] What Maggie Anderson and her family did, we can do one dollar at a time.

- *Our Black Year: One Family's Quest to Buy Black in America's Racially Divided Economy* by Maggie Anderson (New York: Public Affairs, 2012).
- *Black Labor, White Wealth: The Search for Power and Economic Justice* by Claud Anderson (Bethesda, MD: PowerNomics Corporation, 1994).

6. Supporting the Diversity of Strong Black Families

I once heard a pastor say after a man joined the church, "When the man gets saved, the family gets saved." I sat there thinking about how I didn't grow up with my father and at that time my father was with his fifth wife. So was the pastor saying, when my father gives his life to Christ, that was going to help me, my mother, and my siblings?

The African American church can't afford to privilege one family arrangement over another—not in God's economy or in the world's. We have to support the family in the myriad expressions we find in our community, which means we have to stop devaluing families that are headed by women or by same-gender couples. The church that supports families builds ministry with families in mind, ministry that walks along beside them and recognizes how hard it is to have a strong, stable family in times of educational and economic uncertainty.

When families are supported by strong civic and cultural groups, quality schools, intergenerational relationships, and family-sustaining, career-track employment, they thrive. To save a family is to be engaged in being an activist that ensures families have support across the board in order to survive. Parenting classes are part of the answer, but they are not the only answer. Parents also need an education and a job to support the family we are trying to teach them to raise.

- *Climbing Jacob's Ladder: The Enduring Legacies of African-American Families* by Andrew Billingsley (New York: Touchstone, 1994).
- *Ensuring Inequality: The Structural Transformation of the African American Family* by Donna L. Franklin (New York: Oxford University Press, 1997).

7. Where Is the Health?
Healthcare and the African American Community

Access to quality healthcare is essential for a healthy community. There clearly is a crisis in the area of healthcare in the African American community. If you live on the side of town that I live on, you can see it.

> Some characteristics of this African American health crisis include persistent segregation of the health system along race and class lines; race- and class-based inequities and inequalities endemic to each structural component of the health system, the origin of which is over 375 years old; significant race- and class-based health outcome and health status disparities—many of which are worsening;[13]

The reality is that many of our people don't have access to insurance, and thus their healthcare choices are limited economically and geographically. The ripple affect is that this also shapes who serves them because the doctors who practice in working-class African American communities are also shortchanged.

> These patients are automatically forced into publicly financed health facilities or into charity care. Because of the composition of their practices, minority physicians—who disproportionately

practice in poor neighborhoods—have high numbers of Medicaid, uninsured, and poor patients. As a result, they are often excluded or purged from hospital staffs and health maintenance organization (HMO) provider lists as a form of economic credentialing and managed care's avoidance of indigent or severely ill patients. Unfair, discriminatory, often economically driven HMO and hospital staff peer review thwarts quality assurance mechanisms, transforming them into tools to decrease the number of nonpaying, extremely sick, and poor patients (categories disproportionately overrepresented in Black and disadvantaged minority communities) utilizing the HMO and their affiliated hospitals. On the professional level, Black, Hispanic, and dark-skinned foreign physicians . . . are often subjected to these troubling scenarios in the course of caring for their patients.[14]

This is the reality we are dealing with as our people are then forced into overworked, understaffed, overcrowded hospitals and their health problems only worsen.

- *An American Health Dilemma: A Medical History of African Americans and the Problem of Race: Beginnings to 1900* by W. Michael Byrd and Linda A. Clayton (New York: Routledge, 2000).
- *An American Health Dilemma: Race, Medicine, and Health Care in the United States, 1900–2000* by W. Michael Byrd and Linda A. Clayton (New York: Routledge, 2001).
- *Health Disparities in the United States: Social Class, Race, Ethnicity, and Health* by Donald A. Barr (Baltimore: John Hopkins University Press, 2008).

8. Where Are My People?
The Next Generation of Leaders

The church has to walk with young adults as they birth the next movement. What history tells us is that it is the young idealist who will always make the next radical move. Our role as elders is to not get in their way but to make a way and amplify their voice. The key to this next movement should be the spiritual centers of our community. The church has to once again become that place where young adults are nurtured to be leaders of the next movement for the rights and advancement of our people.

What Afeni Shakur, the mother of Tupac Shakur, tells us is that once the civil rights/black power movement moved out of the church, it had a problem. A former Black Panther, Afeni Shakur makes it plain when she says,

> We lost it. We dropped the ball. We didn't know what we were dealing with. We were in over our heads. And, worst of all, we were not listening. We were not listening to the old people. We had removed any semblance of spirituality from our movement. So, when the danger came, what did we have? . . . Not having a spiritual base, not acknowledging the greatness of God, not saying we can't do this without God, we had no solid ground. Instead, we turned against God, and how you gonna win like that?[15]

It is the old people's job to lead in building relationships with the young people by loving them, hearing them, and making room for them. We have to build genuine relationships rooted in love so that we can hear one another. What we also know is that they and we need the church to be the catalyst for this move. In Martin Luther King's last full-length book, he asked, Where will we go, chaos or community? We should revisit his question and build community and allow our young adults to lead us as we walk along beside them.

- *Where Do We Go from Here: Chaos or Community* by Martin Luther King Jr. (Boston: Beacon Press, 2010).
- *Black Against Empire: The History and Politics of the Black Panther Party* by Joshua Bloom and Waldo E. Martin Jr. (Berkeley: University of California Press, 2013).

9. The Digital Divide: From Access to Participation

The digital divide in its simplest form is about access or lack thereof to the Internet. What we know is that those who are in certain parts of a city or who don't have the economic means to afford Internet access are cut out of the loop. To be cut out of the loop means they don't have access to information or opportunity. With most jobs and other means of connection being mediated through the Internet, those who don't have access don't have contact. They are isolated geographically based on where they live, and they are isolated virtually based on not having access to the connected world in which we live.

Not only is this divide about access to information and opportunity, but it is also about how well we can or can't participate in the virtual world. To be heard, seen, and recognized in the virtual world is based on how well we can present ourselves and our work in that world. So this divide is both access and participation, and this is where the future lies for all communities. If we are going to be involved in shaping the future, we have to be part of the digital conversation. The shaping of this next world will be "real virtual" as the virtual and the face-to-face world become one.

- *The Digital Divide: The Internet and Social Inequality in International Perspective*, edited by Massimo Ragnedda and Glenn W. Muschert (New York: Routledge, 2013).
- *The Young and the Digital: What the Migration to Social-Network Sites, Games, and Anytime, Anywhere Media Means for Our Future* by S. Craig Watkins (Boston: Beacon Press, 2010).

10. Pick an Issue: What Is Yours?

Finally, what is your issue? What is missing from the top of my priorities? It is your right to develop your own agenda. You and your congregation can decide how you will act, when you will act, and what will be your first steps. And don't be surprised if your agenda is often in flux as new issues rise to the surface. For example, in your context immigration might be one of your top issues. Immigration is one of the most sensitive issues that the church has to look at from many perspectives. When we think about our sisters and brothers from Asia, Latin America, Africa, and elsewhere around the globe who long to call the United States of America home, how do we walk along beside them and help secure the legal status of citizenship? And how does their presence change our conversations around race and culture in the United States?

This is just one example among many. Don't hesitate to localize your list as you engage mine. It is going to be important to stay informed and connected to what is happening on the ground. This may mean developing a ministry of public information and community relations. You may have a ministry that attends city council meetings, city planning meetings, school board meetings, and other community and public forums and reports to the congregation on a regular basis. Congregations that are going to be effective in leading justice changes in their cities will have to be connected to local leaders in the civic, governmental, and private sectors. We have to be the lobbyist for our communities.

For congregations to be connected with their communities geographically (face-to-face) and virtually is going to take work. It is going to be important to make this a priority in ministry and make sure we are in touch with the heartbeat of the masses. To be informed and provide leadership with the people is hard work. This chapter is really a call to do the work. We are going to have read, to be engaged at the local level, and to be in touch with people's stories. This is the work that has to be done if we hope to be relevant and make a difference. This book and this chapter are only the beginning!

Notes

1. Gerald D. McKnight, *The Last Crusade: Martin Luther King, Jr., the FBI, and the Poor People's Campaign* (Boulder, CO: Westview Press, 1998), 51.
2. Michael Eric Dyson, *April 4, 1968: Martin Luther King Jr.'s Death and How It Changed America* (New York: Basic Civitas Books 2008), 126.
3. Dyson, 120.
4. Sheryl Cashin, *The Failures of Integration: How Race and Class Are Undermining the American Dream* (New York: Public Affairs, 2004), 115.
5. bell hooks, *Where We Stand: Class Matters* (New York: Routledge, 2000), 7.
6. hooks, 101.
7. hooks, 108–9.
8. Michelle Alexander, *The New Jim Crow: Mass Incarceration in the Age of Colorblindness* (New York: The New Press, 2010), 2.
9. Alexander, 7.
10. Dyson, 96.
11. Maggie Anderson, *Our Black Year: One Family's Quest to Buy Black in America's Racially Divided Economy* (New York: Public Affairs, 2012).
12. Anderson, xii.
13. W. Michael Byrd and Linda A. Crawford, *An American Health Dilemma: A Medical History of African Americans and the Problem of Race: Beginnings to 1900* (New York: Routledge, 2000), xxiv.
14. Byrd and Crawford, xxv–xxvi.
15. Jasmine Guy, *Afeni Shakur: Evolution of a Revolutionary* (New York: Atria Books, 2004), 67–68.

Afterword

Ralph Watkins and Justin West challenge readers to engage in a balanced discourse that takes seriously variant perspectives on the question, "Is the black church dead or alive?" This question resounds across the American landscape, expressed through academic discourses, in day-to-day conversations, and through the often unspoken critiques of those who choose not to engage the black church for various reasons. Watkins and West attempt to move these perspectives away from polemical arguments that overlook the vitality of black congregations in diverse sociopolitical, geographic, and theological "camps," while acknowledging the very real struggles of black churches on the brink of death.

As an author and scholar who has for a long time had his finger on the pulse, not only of the black church but of the hip-hop generation, Watkins is well equipped to further initiate and engage in this dialogue. His conversations around issues impacting local and global communities contribute to much-needed discourses related to theology and its relevance in the twenty-first century. Particularly powerful is his exploration of the potential for bridging the gap between prophetic black church traditions and contemporary praise-and-worship-oriented megachurch trends.

Beginning by establishing criteria for "being church," engaging the voices of Gayraud Wilmore, James Cone, and others, Watkins' assertion is clear that the black church must be a community with a mission related to liberation through an African American spirituality that embraces its history and legacy. As Jacquelyn Grant reminds us, in order to be so, the black church must also look at its legacy of exclusion in regard to the majority of its constituents, namely black women. Black women's voices must be heard and their presence invited to tables of discourse when engaging any critical discourse related to the life and identity of the church. Further, the state of black women should be central to any assessment and outcome related to the church's condition, alive or dead, as it directly correlates to the real, lived experiences of those who constitute it. And in chapter 7, noting the imperative need to address the intersections of racism, sexism, classism, mass incarceration, several other societal ills and the public policies that under gird them, Watkins contends that churches need to embrace a black feminist and womanist stance and face head-on issues that plague the black church and community.

The Future of the African American Church is a useful read for the academician and the churched and "unchurched" layperson alike. Highlighting issues that impact the daily wrestlings of the black church and community at-large, the text lifts the problematic realities that reach a wide range of readers. Through a *Sankofan* method, which looks back at some "best practices" in order to create a viable present and future, this volume raises questions rather than providing rigid and exhaustive answers. Watkins and West point readers toward pertinent and pivotal concerns that, if engaged, potentially foster the kinds of conciliatory words and deeds that can bridge gaps across differences in black churches.

Maisha I. K. Handy, PhD
Associate Vice President of Academic Services/Academic Dean
Associate Professor of Christian Education
Interdenominational Theological Center

Epilogue

I have written the foreword for a dozen different volumes over my career, usually to recommend the book and urge potential buyers and readers to proceed with what lies ahead, and also to commend the author for the insights and contributions that the book offers. However, this is my first afterword, or epilogue. In this instance, the book has already been read, and readers have now reached their own conclusions about its contents and contributions. What does an outside voice, someone other than the authors say at this point?

What I have concluded is that an epilogue is not a critical review of the book. Every book promises to engage topics, answer questions, and bring added clarity to complicated issues. This book by Ralph Watkins and Julian West is no exception. I will let readers and future reviewers determine if the book has delivered on what it promised, especially as it explores the tension between prophetic and praise churches as a way to envision the future of the black church in America.

My caution in writing this epilogue is also informed by the fact that this book began with something of a critique of one of my own books, *Where Have All the Prophets Gone?* However, just as I will not attempt to review this book, so I will also refrain here from offering a rebuttal in my own defense. Once again, I will leave it to the readers to determine the merits of the critique made by Watkins and West. My epilogue will pursue a different course.

What I will offer here are three brief observations. First, I observe that this book is part of an ongoing challenge for the church universal about how to keep the message of the gospel alive and relevant from one generation to the next. This challenge is especially relevant as that gospel and the people to whom it is being presented are confronted with swift and startling changes in culture, religious diversity, and the loss of historical memory and identity. What West and Watkins are exploring may be focused on the future of the African American church in the twenty-first century, but the same issues of theological focus, relevant forms of ministry, inherited historical traditions and practices of worship and service, are being raised by Christians of all denominations and cultural identities all over the world. No one book can resolve all of these questions, but this book is an attempt to be part of what is an ongoing global conversation. This book has much to say about how the African American church can navigate the future that awaits it in its many denominational and theological forms.

Second, I observe that this book does an admirable job of addressing the question that is as old as Micah 6:8, "What does the Lord require of us?" In the end, the church must be sure that its understanding of its ministry is informed by and rooted in some clear and inescapable biblical mandate. Why one church focuses much of its ministry on working for God's people residing outside its walls, while another church spends much of its time worshipping God within its walls usually comes down to some biblical argument concerning "What does God require of us?" Thus, this book is a reminder that every church needs to look at itself and look at the community in which it is situated and ask the question of Micah, "What does the Lord require of us?" The question is not what do we want to do, or what is easiest for us to do, but what does God expect us to do. That is a conversation every church needs to have with itself as we face the future. The words of Psalm 127:1 should never be far from the minds of pastors and those attempting to plan for the future of the church: "Unless the Lord builds the house, those that build it labor in vain" (NRSV).

My third and final observation comes in the form of a question: Is there and should there ever be a choice to be made between prophetic and praise churches? Can we really be the church without speaking truth to power or advocating on behalf of the least of these? Conversely, is it possible to be the church without taking time to worship God, in spirit and in truth? After all, our worship declares that our God is able to tear down walls of division, to set the captives free, and to bring down the mighty from their thrones. Our worship of God is not solely because we need a blessing or a healing or some other personal intervention from the Almighty.

Worship in the African American church has long viewed God in a much broader and deeper context.

The spirituals got it right when they cried out, "Didn't my Lord deliver Daniel, and why not every man?" And when they sang, God's "got the whole world in his hands," hasn't that been the hope and faith of the African American church from its infancy in the eighteenth century? "The Lord will make a way somehow," we proclaim, not just for any one of us as we move through the trials of our individual lives, but for all of as we continue the journey from slavery, sharecropping, segregation, and second-class citizenship to full freedom in this land.

Watkins and West helped to make this point when they lifted up the ministry of Trinity United Church of Christ in Chicago as an exemplary prophetic church. However, anyone who has ever visited Trinity UCC knows the power and fervor of the worship experience there. Let us not create or exacerbate difference and divisions about prophetic and praise churches. Instead, let us worship in the church *and* work in the world, for the God who is revealed in Jesus Christ calls us to take up the cross and follow him!

Marvin A. McMickle, MDiv, PhD
President, Colgate Rochester Crozer Divinity School
Rochester, New York